Dumpling Pups

Crochet & Collect Them All!

Sarah Sloyer

Dover Publications, Inc.
Mineola, New York

Copyright

Copyright © 2018 by Sarah Sloyer
All rights reserved.

Bibliographical Note

Dumpling Pups: Crochet and Collect Them All! is a new work, first published by Dover Publications, Inc., in 2018.

Library of Congress Cataloging-in-Publication Data

Names: Sloyer, Sarah, author.
Title: Dumpling pups : crochet and collect them all! / Sarah Sloyer.
Description: Mineola, New York : Dover Publications, Inc., 2018. | Includes
   bibliographical references and index.
Identifiers: LCCN 2018002659| ISBN 9780486821481 (alk. paper) | ISBN
   048682148X (alk. paper)
Subjects: LCSH: Crocheting—Patterns. | Soft toy making—Patterns. |
   Dogs—Miscellanea.
Classification: LCC TT829 .S57 2018 | DDC 746.43/4—dc23
LC record available at https://lccn.loc.gov/2018002659

Manufactured in the United States by LSC Communications
82148X01   2018
www.doverpublications.com

TECHNIQUES (U.S. terms)

BLO; back loops only: Work through only the back loops for as long as instructed.

Ch; chain: With a slipknot on your hook, yarn over and pull through.

Change color: When instructed to change colors, insert hook into stitch. Yarn over and pull through with your original color so there are two loops on your hook. Then, take your new color and pull it through both loops on your hook. Remember: this counts as one single crochet stitch! Continue with new color.

   Note: When changing colors, cut previous color and tie your yarn tails in a knot.

Dc; double crochet: Wrap working yarn over hook, insert into stitch, yarn over and pull through so there are three loops on your hook. Yarn over and pull through two loops, then yarn over and pull through all loops on hook to complete stitch.

Dec; single crochet invisible decrease: Insert hook through the front loops of the next two stitches. Yarn over and pull through so there are two loops on your hook. Yarn over and pull through both loops to complete decrease.

Embroidery: All pieces show eyes/noses/features embroidered with DMC embroidery floss (3 strands). All eyes and noses were created by making approximately 10 stitches, but you can embroider your features as thick as you would like.

Fasten off: Slip stitch. After you finish your slip stitch, you'll need to fasten off the yarn and secure it so the stitch will not unravel. Cut the yarn leaving a few inches of tail. Then, with your hook, draw the tail through the loop on your hook. Remove hook and pull on tail to tighten. With a yarn needle, weave the tail through the stitches of the fabric to hide it.

Finished Size: Keep in mind that the finished size may vary depending on your hook size, yarn type, and tension.

FLO; front loops only: Work through only the front loops for as long as instructed.

HDC; half double crochet: Wrap working yarn over hook, insert into stitch, yarn over and pull through so there are three loops on your hook. Yarn over and pull through all three loops to complete stitch.

Hook Size Used: D-3/3.25mm

Inc; single crochet increase: Make two single crochet stitches in the same stitch.

Marker placement: Your stitch marker is always placed in the first stitch of every round. When starting an oval piece, work the foundation chain as instructed, then place the marker in the first stitch that you work back into the foundation chain.

Parentheses; ( ): Work the stitches within the parentheses as many times as instructed.

Project Gauge: Not crucial for these patterns as long as all stitches are tight enough to conceal the stuffing inside.

Sc; single crochet: Insert hook into stitch, yarn over, pull through so you have two loops on your hook. Yarn over and pull through both loops to complete stitch.

Sl st; slip stitch: Insert hook into next stitch. Yarn over and pull through the loop on your hook. If fastening off, cut yarn and pull through.

Whipstitch: Hold the two sides of crochet to be joined so the stitches on either side are lined up with one another. With your yarn tail threaded onto a needle, weave the needle through each set of stitches once, moving onto the next set and repeating until all stitches have been joined.

Working in the Round: When working in rounds, pieces are worked in a continuous spiral (no joining of rounds).

   Note: Some pieces have a small number of stitches in each round (especially legs) and can be tiny and fiddly to work with—take your time, and always remember to take breaks and stretch your hands!

contents

Griffin the Corgi
1

Lincoln the Dachshund
4

Bella the Chocolate Lab
8

Newt the Yellow Lab
12

Talulah the Chihuahua
16

Dog Bowls
19

Blossom the Pug
22

Dog Bed
25

Decker the Bernese
Mountain Dog **28**

Saatchi the Shiba Inu
32

Wendy the Boston
Terrier **36**

Victor the Bull Terrier
40

Bonus Pattern!

Bonus Pattern!

contents

Cookie the Jack Russell
Terrier **44**

Pappy the Scottish
Terrier **48**

Boris the Husky
52

Malcolm the Standard
Poodle **56**

Buck the Pug
60

Duncan the Golden
Retriever **64**

Bonus
Pattern!

Cardboard Box
68

Mack the Bulldog
70

Bonus
Pattern!

Dog Bone
74

Bruiser the Greyhound
76

Morty the French
Bulldog **80**

Cole the Black Lab
84

griffin

Breed: Pembroke Welsh Corgi

Griffin is the youngest out of all the pups, and as a result, he has boundless energy and enthusiasm for just about everything, especially board games. He has an extensive collection of them in the closet under the stairs, and loves hosting weekly game nights (as long as everyone follows the rules). He has a weird habit of eating bananas with the peels still on.

FINISHED SIZE: 3½in/9cm tall
SKILL LEVEL: Intermediate
MATERIALS

- Lion Brand® Vanna's Choice® 3.5oz/100g, 170yds/156m (100% acrylic)—one skein each: #860-100 White (Color A), #860-130 Honey (Color B)
- Size D-3 (3.25mm) crochet hook
- Yarn needle
- Embroidery needle
- Black embroidery floss (for eyes and nose)
- Polyester stuffing
- Wooden stuffing stick
- Stitch markers and pins

Muzzle

In Color A:

Rnd 1: Ch 3. Starting in second ch from hook, sc 1. In next st, sc 4. On opposite side of foundation ch, sc 4 into next st—9 sts.

Rnds 2–3: Sc in all 9 sts—9 sts.

Fasten off with a sl st, leaving a tail for assembly. Embroider nose.

Head and Body

*Head and body are started in Color B. **Sections shown in purple** are completed in Color A. See "Changing Colors" in the Techniques section for more information on how to change yarn colors.*

In Color B, except where noted:

Rnd 1: Ch 3. Starting in second ch from hook, sc 1. In next st, sc 4. On opposite side of foundation ch, sc 4 into next st—9 sts.

Rnd 2: Sc 2, inc, sc 3 into next st, sc 3, sc 3 into next st, inc—15 sts.

Rnd 3: Sc 4, inc in next 3 sts, sc 4, inc in next 3 sts, sc 1—21 sts.

Rnd 4: Sc in all 21 sts—21 sts.

Rnd 5: Sc 3, inc, (sc 6, inc) 2 times, sc 3—24 sts.

Rnds 6–9: Sc in all 24 sts—24 sts.

Rnd 10: Sc 3, ch 6. Starting in second ch from hook, place a new marker and sc 5 back down to base of ch. The new marker will now be the beginning of your rounds. Remove your original marker. When you reach the base of the ch, continue working into the next sts in the round normally: sc 6, **sc 12**, sc 10, working your way back up the other side of the ch, sc 4 into last st before marker—37 sts.

Rnd 11: Sc 11, **sc 12,** sc 14—37 sts.

Rnd 12: (Inc, sc 1) 3 times, sc 5, **sc 12,** sc 7, (inc, sc 1) 3 times, sc 1—43 sts.

Rnd 13: Sc 14, **sc 12,** sc 16, inc—44 sts.

Rnd 14: Sc 14, **sc 12,** sc 18—44 sts.

Rnd 15: Change to Color A in first st. Remainder of rnds are worked in Color A. Sc 8, dec, (sc 9, dec) 3 times—40 sts.

Rnd 16: Sc in all 40 sts—40 sts.

Rnd 17: Sc 4, dec, (sc 8, dec) 3 times, sc 4—36 sts. Begin stuffing the head.

Rnd 18: Sc 5, dec, (sc 10, dec) 2 times, sc 5—33 sts.

Rnd 19: (Sc 9, dec) 3 times—30 sts.

Rnd 20: (Sc 3, dec) 6 times—24 sts.

Rnd 21: Sc 1, dec, (sc 2, dec) 5 times, sc 1—18 sts. Stuff the body generously, continuing to stuff firmly as you finish the following rounds.

Rnd 22: (Sc 1, dec) 6 times—12 sts.

Rnd 23: Dec 6 times—6 sts.

Fasten off with a sl st, leaving a tail. Using a yarn needle, thread the tail through each of the front loops of the remaining 6 sts, pulling tightly to close hole. Weave in and trim yarn.

Legs (Make 4)

In Color A:

Rnd 1: Start 6 sc in an adjustable ring—6 sts.

Rnds 2–3: Sc in all 6 sts—6 sts.

Fasten off with a sl st, leaving a tail for assembly. Do not stuff.

Ears (Make 2)

In Color B:

Rnd 1: Start 6 sc in an adjustable ring—6 sts.

Rnd 2: Sc in all 6 sts—6 sts.

Rnd 3: (Sc 2, inc) 2 times—8 sts.

Rnd 4: (Sc 3, inc) 2 times—10 sts.

Rnd 5: Sc 4, inc, sc 5—11 sts.

Rnds 6–8: Sc in all 11 sts—11 sts.

Fasten off with a sl st, leaving a tail for assembly. Do not stuff. Press flat and pinch sides of ear together as shown to give the ear its shape, running the yarn tail through the bottom of the ear to help it hold its shape.

ASSEMBLY

Parts can be assembled in whichever order you choose, as shown. Stuff muzzle lightly.

lincoln

Breed: Dachshund

Lincoln is a stylish city dog, and the only pup in the bunch to have figured out how to use the internet. He's never far from his laptop or smartphone, and he has an impressive following on social media. Lincoln is a very handsome fellow—after all, he just wants to share himself with the world!

FINISHED SIZE: 3½in/9cm tall

SKILL LEVEL: Intermediate

MATERIALS

- Lion Brand® Vanna's Choice® 3.5oz/100g, 170yds/156m (100% acrylic)—one skein: #860-124 Toffee
- Size D-3 (3.25mm) crochet hook
- Yarn needle
- Embroidery needle
- Black embroidery floss (for eyes and nose)
- Polyester stuffing
- Wooden stuffing stick
- Stitch markers and pins

Head

Rnd 1: Start 6 sc in an adjustable ring—6 sts.

Rnd 2: Sc in all 6 sts—6 sts.

Rnd 3: Sc 1, inc, sc 4—7 sts.

Rnd 4: Sc 1, (sc 3 into next st) 2 times, sc 4—11 sts.

Rnd 5: Sc in all 11 sts—11 sts.

Rnd 6: Sc 1, inc, sc 3, sc 3 into next st, sc 2, inc, sc 2—15 sts.

Rnd 7: Sc in all 15 sts—15 sts.

Rnd 8: Sc 2, (inc, sc 1) 5 times, sc 3—20 sts.

Rnd 9: Sc 5, (inc, sc 1) 5 times, sc 5—25 sts. Embroider eyes and nose.

Rnds 10–11: Sc in all 25 sts—25 sts.

Rnd 12: Sc 2, inc, (sc 4, inc) 4 times, sc 2—30 sts.

Rnd 13: Sc in all 30 sts—30 sts.

Rnd 14: Sc 2, dec, (sc 4, dec) 4 times, sc 2—25 sts.

Rnd 15: (Sc 3, dec) 5 times—20 sts. Begin stuffing the head, continuing to stuff firmly as you finish the following rounds.

Rnd 16: Sc 1, dec, (sc 2, dec) 4 times, sc 1—15 sts.

Rnd 17: (Sc 1, dec) 5 times—10 sts.

Rnd 18: Dec 5 times—5 sts.

Fasten off with a sl st, leaving a tail. Using a yarn needle, thread the tail through each of the front loops of the remaining 5 sts, pulling tightly to close hole. Weave in and trim yarn.

Body

Rnd 1: Ch 12, making sure to leave a long tail (at least 8 in) while making your slipknot. Insert hook into first ch and pull through a sl st to join the two ends of the chain.

Rnd 2: Sc in all 12 sts—12 sts.

Rnd 3: Sc 1, ch 10. Starting in second ch from hook, place a new marker. This will be the new beginning of your round. Remove your original marker. Continue: sc 29, sc 4 into last st before marker—33 sts.

Rnd 4: Inc, sc 32—34 sts.

Rnd 5: (Sc 3, inc) 2 times, (sc 5, inc) 3 times, sc 3, inc, sc 4—40 sts.

Rnds 6–8: Sc in all 40 sts—40 sts.

Rnd 9: (Sc 3, dec) 2 times, (sc 5, dec) 3 times, sc 3, dec, sc 2, dec—33 sts.

Rnd 10: Dec, sc 13, dec 2 times, sc 12, dec—29 sts.

Rnd 11: Dec, sc 11, dec 3 times, sc 8, dec—24 sts.

Rnd 12: Dec, stop and do not complete rest of round—23 sts. Stuff body lightly.

Fasten off with a sl st, leaving a tail. Use tail to stitch the bottom of the body shut, as shown. Weave in and trim yarn. Finish stuffing the body firmly through the neck opening.

Ears (Make 2)

Rnd 1: Start 6 sc in an adjustable ring—6 sts.

Rnd 2: Inc 6 times—12 sts.

Rnd 3: Sc in all 12 sts—12 sts.

Rnd 4: (Sc 4, dec) 2 times—10 sts.

Rnd 5: Sc in all 10 sts—10 sts.

Rnd 6: (Sc 3, dec) 2 times—8 sts.

Rnd 7: Sc in all 8 sts—8 sts.

Do not fasten off or stuff; remove marker, press flat and close top with 3 sc as shown. Yarn over and pull through to fasten off, leaving a tail for sewing.

Legs (Make 4)

Rnd 1: Start 5 sc in an adjustable ring—5 sts.

Rnds 2–3: Sc in all 5 sts—5 sts.

Fasten off with a sl st, leaving a tail for assembly. Do not stuff.

Tail

Row 1: Ch 9, making sure to leave a long tail (8in) while making your slipknot.

Row 2: Starting in second ch from hook, sl st, sc 7.

Yarn over and pull through to fasten off, leaving a tail for sewing.

ASSEMBLY

Attach the head to the body as shown.

After head is attached to body, sew on the remainder of the parts in whichever order you choose.

bella

Breed: Chocolate Labrador Retriever (Chocolate Lab)

Even when Bella was small, she was, well, *large*. Ever since she was a young pup, Bella has dreamed of being a prima ballerina. Though naysayers have always told her she is too big-boned, Bella is determined to realize her dream, no matter her size, or the fact that she's a dog—and she totally rocks her tutu while doing it.

Fasten off with a sl st, leaving a tail for assembly. Embroider nose.

FINISHED SIZE: 5in/12.5cm tall

SKILL LEVEL: Intermediate

MATERIALS

- Lion Brand® Vanna's Choice® 3.5oz/100g, 170yds/156m (100% acrylic)—one skein each: #860-126 Chocolate (Color A), #860-101 Pink (Color B)
- Size D-3 (3.25mm) crochet hook
- Yarn needle
- Embroidery needle
- Light brown embroidery floss (for nose and eyes)
- Polyester stuffing
- Wooden stuffing stick
- Stitch markers and pins

Ears (Make 2)

In Color A:

Rnd 1: Start 6 sc in an adjustable ring—6 sts.

Rnd 2: (Sc 1, inc) 3 times—9 sts.

Rnd 3: (Sc 2, inc) 3 times—12 sts.

Rnd 4: Sc in all 12 sts—12 sts.

Rnd 5: (Sc 2, dec) 3 times—9 sts.

Rnd 6: Sc in all 9 sts—9 sts.

Rnd 7: (Sc 1, dec) 3 times—6 sts.

Do not fasten off or stuff; press flat and close top with 3 sc. Yarn over and pull through to fasten off, leaving a tail for assembly.

Muzzle

In Color A:

Rnd 1: Ch 4. Starting in second ch from hook, sc 2, sc 4 into next st. On opposite side of foundation ch, sc 1, sc 4 into next st—11 sts.

Rnd 2: Sc 3, sc 3 into next st, inc, sc 4, inc, sc 3 in next st—17 sts.

Head and Body

In Color A:

Rnd 1: Ch 5. Starting in second ch from hook, sc 3. In next st, sc 4. On opposite side of foundation ch, sc 2, sc 4 into next st—13 sts.

Rnd 2: Sc 4, sc 3 into next st, inc, sc 5, inc, sc 3 into next st—19 sts.

Rnd 3: Sc 5, inc 3 times, sc 7, inc 3 times, sc 1—25 sts.

Rnd 4: Sc 6, (inc, sc 1) 3 times, sc 7, (inc, sc 1) 3 times—31 sts.

Rnd 5: Sc 7, (inc, sc 2) 3 times, sc 6, (inc, sc 2) 3 times—37 sts.

Rnds 6–7: Sc in all 37 sts—37 sts.

Rnd 8: Sc 8, (inc, sc 3) 3 times, sc 6, (inc, sc 3) 2 times, inc, sc 2—43 sts.

Rnd 9: Sc 40, change to Color B in next st, sc 2—43 sts.

Rnd 10: Sc 10, (inc, sc 2) 3 times, sc 12, (inc, sc 2) 3 times, sc 3—49 sts.

Rnd 11: Sc in all 49 sts—49 sts.

Rnd 12: Sc 2, dec, (sc 4, dec) 7 times, sc 3—41 sts.

Rnd 13: (Sc 3, dec) 8 times, sc 1—33 sts.

Pin muzzle to head to determine eye placement. Embroider eyes.

Rnd 14: Sc in all 33 sts—33 sts.

Rnd 15: Sc 5, inc, (sc 10, inc) 2 times, sc 5—36 sts.

Rnd 16: (Sc 11, inc) 3 times—39 sts.

Rnd 17: Sc 8, inc, (sc 9, inc) 3 times—43 sts.

Rnd 18: Sc 4, inc, (sc 6, inc) 5 times, sc 3—49 sts.

Rnds 19–21: Sc in all 49 sts—49 sts.

Rnd 22: (Sc 7, inc) 6 times, sc 1—55 sts.

Rnds 23–25: Sc in all 55 sts—55 sts.

Rnd 26: Sc 5, inc, (sc 10, inc) 4 times, sc 5—60 sts.

Rnd 27: Sc in all 60 sts, changing to Color B in last st—60 sts.

Rnd 28: In FLO: sc in all 60 sts—60 sts. When you reach the end of the round, drop Color B from your hook and place a marker in the loop to hold your place. In remaining back loop of Rnd 28, place a new marker and continue in Color A.

Rnds 29–31: Sc in all 60 sts—60 sts.

Rnd 32: Sc 5, dec, (sc 10, dec) 4 times, sc 5—55 sts.

Rnd 33: (Sc 9, dec) 5 times—50 sts.

Begin stuffing the head and body, continuing to stuff as you finish the remaining rounds.

Rnd 34: (Sc 3, dec) 10 times—40 sts.

Rnd 35: Sc 1, dec, (sc 2, dec) 9 times, sc 1—30 sts.

Rnd 36: (Sc 1, dec) 10 times—20 sts.

Rnd 37: Dec 10 times—10 sts.

Rnd 38: Dec 5 times—5 sts.

Fasten off with a sl st, leaving a tail. Using a yarn needle, thread the tail through each of the front loops of the remaining 5 sts, pulling tightly to close hole. Weave in and trim yarn.

Front Legs (Make 2)

In Color A:

Rnd 1: Start 6 sc in an adjustable ring—6 sts.

Rnd 2: (Sc 1, inc) 3 times—9 sts.

Rnds 3–6: Sc in all 9 sts—9 sts.

Do not fasten off. Stuff lightly, remove marker, press flat and insert hook through both sides to close top with 2 sc. Yarn over and pull through to fasten off, leaving a tail for sewing.

Back Legs (Make 2)

Rnd 1: Start 6 sc in an adjustable ring—6 sts.

Rnd 2: Inc 6 times—6 sts.

Rnds 3–5: Sc in all 6 sts—6 sts.

Fasten off with a sl st, leaving a tail for sewing. Stuff firmly.

Tail (Make 2, then join)

In Color A:

Row 1: Ch 11, making sure to leave a long tail (12in) while making your slipknot.

Row 2: Starting in second ch from hook, sc 5, hdc 5.

Yarn over and pull through to fasten off, leaving a tail for sewing. Sandwich the two tail pieces together so the sts are aligned and use one of the remaining tails to whipstitch the pieces together, down both sides. Weave in and trim remaining tails, leaving one for assembly later.

Tutu

Before beginning the tutu, determine where you will want your front legs placed. The legs will be stitched to the body between Rnds 28–29. Pin the legs to the body, making sure they are centered with the other features (head and eyes). When you are happy with their placement, continue:

Pick up the loop of Color B you dropped in Rnd 28 and continue working. Work 5 dc in each st around, until you reach where you want the first front leg to be placed. Sl st 8, then continue to work 5 dc in each of the following sts until you reach the second leg. Sl st 8, then continue to work 5 dc until you reach the end of the round. Yarn over and pull through to fasten off, then weave in tail.

ASSEMBLY

Parts can be assembled in whichever order you choose, as shown.

newt

Breed: Yellow Labrador Retriever (Yellow Lab)

Compared to her big sister Bella, Newt is rather petite—she also doesn't share her sibling's dream of becoming a prima ballerina, or any other kind of dancer or athlete. In fact, right now, Newt aspires to nap as much as possible. Even though they have different priorities, Newt and Bella still support one another unconditionally in their goals, as sisters do!

Zzz

FINISHED SIZE: 2½in/6.5cm tall

SKILL LEVEL: Easy

MATERIALS

- Lion Brand® Vanna's Choice® 3.5oz/100g, 170yds/156m (100% acrylic)—one skein: #860-123 Beige
- Size D-3 (3.25mm) crochet hook
- Yarn needle
- Embroidery needle
- Black embroidery floss (for eyes and nose)
- Polyester stuffing
- Wooden stuffing stick
- Stitch markers and pins

Head and Body

Rnd 1: Ch 4. Starting in second ch from hook, sc 2. In next st, sc 4. On opposite side of foundation ch, sc 1, sc 4 into next st—11 sts.

Rnds 2–3: Sc in all 11 sts—11 sts.

Rnd 4: (Sc 3 into next st) 4 times, (sc 1, inc) 3 times, sc 1—22 sts.

Rnd 5: Sc in all 22 sts—22 sts.

Rnd 6: Sc 1, (sc 3 into next st, sc 2) 4 times, sc 9—30 sts.

Rnd 7: Sc in all 30 sts—30 sts.

Rnd 8: Sc 2, (inc, sc 3) 5 times, sc 4, inc, sc 3—36 sts. Embroider eyes and nose.

Rnds 9–12: Sc in all 36 sts—36 sts.

Rnd 13: (Sc 11, inc) 3 times—39 sts.

Rnd 14: Sc in all 39 sts—39 sts.

Rnd 15: Sc 6, inc, (sc 12, inc) 2 times, sc 6—42 sts.

Rnds 16–17: Sc in all 42 sts—42 sts.

Rnd 18: Sc 6, dec, (sc 12, dec) 2 times, sc 6—39 sts.

Rnd 19: Sc in all 39 sts—39 sts.

Rnd 20: (Sc 11, dec) 3 times—36 sts.

Rnd 21: Sc 2, dec, (sc 4, dec) 5 times, sc 2—30 sts.

Rnd 22: (Sc 3, dec) 6 times—24 sts. Begin stuffing the body generously, continuing to stuff firmly as you finish the following rounds.

Ears (Make 2)

Rnd 1: Start 6 sc in an adjustable ring—6 sts.

Rnd 2: Inc 6 times—12 sts.

Rnd 3: Sc in all 12 sts—12 sts.

Rnd 4: (Sc 4, dec) 2 times—10 sts.

Rnd 5: (Sc 3, dec) 2 times—8 sts.

Rnd 6: Sc 1, dec, sc 2, dec, sc 1—6 sts.

Do not fasten off or stuff; remove marker, press flat and close top with 2 sc as shown. Yarn over and pull through to fasten off, leaving a tail for sewing.

Rnd 23: Sc 1, dec, (sc 2, dec) 5 times, sc 1—18 sts.

Rnd 24: (Sc 1, dec) 6 times—12 sts.

Rnd 25: Dec 6 times—6 sts.

Fasten off with a sl st, leaving a tail. Using a yarn needle, thread the tail through each of the front loops of the remaining 6 sts, pulling tightly to close hole. Weave in and trim yarn.

Legs (Make 4)

Rnd 1: Start 6 sc in an adjustable ring—6 sts.

Rnds 2–3: Sc in all 6 sts—6 sts.

Fasten off with a sl st, leaving a tail for assembly. Do not stuff.

Tail (Make 2, then join)

Row 1: Ch 9, making sure to leave a long tail (8in) while making your slipknot.

Row 2: Starting in second ch from hook, sl st, sc 7.

Yarn over and pull through to fasten off, leaving a tail for sewing. Sandwich the two tail pieces together so the sts are aligned, as shown, and use one of the remaining tails to whipstitch the pieces together, down both sides. Weave in and trim remaining tails, leaving one for assembly later.

ASSEMBLY

Parts can be assembled in whichever order you choose. Place ears as shown.

talulah

Breed: Chihuahua

Although she may be small, Talulah manages to get around the house very quickly—the kitchen in particular! This pint-sized powerhouse is a master chef who delights the rest of the pups with her fabulous (but spicy) cooking. Her signature dish? Thai green curry! (Did you think we were going to say tacos? Nope. Talulah rejects Chihuahua stereotypes.)

FINISHED SIZE: 3in/7.5cm tall

SKILL LEVEL: Easy

MATERIALS

- Lion Brand® Vanna's Choice® 3.5oz/100g, 170yds/156m (100% acrylic)—one skein #860-130 Honey
- Size D-3 (3.25mm) crochet hook
- Yarn needle
- Embroidery needle
- Black embroidery floss (for eyes and nose)
- Polyester stuffing
- Wooden stuffing stick
- Stitch markers and pins

Head

Rnd 1: Start 4 sc in an adjustable ring—4 sts.

Rnd 2: Sc in all 4 sts—4 sts.

Rnd 3: (Sc 3 into next st) 2 times, sc 2—8 sts.

Rnd 4: Sc 2, (sc 3 into next st) 2 times, sc 4—12 sts.

Rnd 5: Sc 4, (sc 3 into next st, sc 1) 3 times, sc 2—18 sts.

Rnd 6: Sc 6, (sc 3 into next st, sc 2) 3 times, sc 3—24 sts.

Rnds 7–8: Sc in all 24 sts—24 sts. Embroider eyes and nose.

Rnd 9: Sc 3, (inc, sc 6) 3 times—27 sts.

Rnds 10–11: Sc in all 27 sts—27 sts.

Rnd 12: Sc 3, (dec, sc 6) 3 times—24 sts.

Rnd 13: Sc in all 24 sts—24 sts.

Rnd 14: Sc 1, dec, (sc 2, dec) 5 times, sc 1—18 sts. Begin stuffing the head generously, continuing to stuff firmly as you finish the following rounds.

Rnd 15: (Sc 1, dec) 6 times—12 sts.

Rnd 16: Dec 6 times—6 sts.

Fasten off with a sl st, leaving a tail. Using a yarn needle, thread the tail through each of the front loops of the remaining 6 sts, pulling tightly to close hole. Weave in and trim yarn.

Body

Rnd 1: Start 6 sc in an adjustable ring—6 sts.

Rnd 2: Inc 6 times—12 sts.

Rnd 3: (Sc 1, inc) 6 times—18 sts.

Rnd 4: Sc in all 18 sts—18 sts.

Rnd 5: (Sc 7, dec) 2 times—16 sts.

Rnd 6: Sc 3, dec, sc 6, dec, sc 3—14 sts.

Rnd 7: (Sc 5, dec) 2 times—12 sts.

Rnd 8: Sc 2, dec, sc 4, dec, sc 2—10 sts.

Rnd 9: Sc 6, dec, sc 2—9 sts.

Fasten off with a sl st, leaving a tail. Stuff body.

Ears (Make 2)

Rnd 1: Start 4 sc in an adjustable ring—4 sts.

Rnd 2: (Sc 1, inc) 2 times—6 sts.

Rnd 3: (Sc 2, inc) 2 times—8 sts.

Rnd 4: (Sc 3, inc) 2 times—10 sts.

Rnd 5: (Sc 4, inc) 2 times—12 sts.

Rnd 6: (Sc 5, inc) 2 times—14 sts.

Rnd 7: (Sc 6, inc) 2 times—16 sts.

Fasten off with a sl st, leaving a tail. Press flat; do not stuff.

Front Legs (Make 2)

Rnd 1: Start 4 sc in an adjustable ring—4 sts.

Rnds 2–4: Sc in all 4 sts—4 sts.

Do not fasten off or stuff; remove marker, press flat and close top with 1 sc as shown. Yarn over and pull through to fasten off, leaving a tail for sewing.

Back Legs (Make 2)

Rnd 1: Start 4 sc in an adjustable ring—4 sts.

Rnds 2–3: Sc in all 4 sts—4 sts.

Do not fasten off or stuff; remove marker, press flat and close top with 1 sc. Yarn over and pull through to fasten off, leaving a tail for sewing.

Tail

Row 1: Ch 6, making sure to leave a long tail (8in) while making your slipknot.

Row 2: Starting in second ch from hook, sl st, sc 4.

Yarn over and pull through to fasten off, leaving a tail for sewing.

ASSEMBLY

Attach the head to the body as shown.

After head is attached to body, sew on the remainder of the parts in whichever order you choose.

dog bowls

Bonus Pattern!

FINISHED SIZE: 1½in/4cm diameter

SKILL LEVEL: Easy

MATERIALS

- Lion Brand® Vanna's Choice® 3.5oz/100g, 170yds/156m (100% acrylic)—one skein each: # 860-180 Cranberry (Color A), #860-115 Light Blue (Color B), #860-176 Peacock (Color C), #860-124 Toffee (Color D)
- Size D-3 (3.25mm) crochet hook
- Yarn needle
- Embroidery needle
- Polyester stuffing
- Wooden stuffing stick
- Stitch markers and pins

Water Bowl

Bowl Top

In Color A:

Rnd 1: Start 6 sc in an adjustable ring—6 sts.

Rnd 2: Inc 6 times—12 sts.

Rnd 3: (Sc 1, inc) 6 times—18 sts.

Rnd 4: Sc 1, inc, (sc 2, inc) 5 times, sc 1—24 sts.

Rnds 5–6: Sc in all 24 sts, changing to Color B at end of Rnd 6—24 sts.

Rnd 7: In FLO: sc in all 24 sts—24 sts.

Drop loop from hook and put a marker in it to save your place. Turn bowl inside out, with wrong side facing out.

Bowl Base

In Color A:

Rnd 1: Start 6 sc in an adjustable ring—6 sts.

Rnd 2: Inc 6 times—12 sts.

Rnd 3: (Sc 1, inc) 6 times—18 sts.

Rnd 4: Sc 1, inc, (sc 2, inc) 5 times, sc 1—24 sts.

Rnd 5: (Sc 5, inc) 4 times—28 sts.

Rnd 6: In BLO: sc in all 28 sts—28 sts.

Rnd 7: Sc 6, dec, sc 12, dec, sc 6—26 sts.

Rnd 8: (Sc 11, dec) 2 times—24 sts.

Do not fasten off. Place bowl top inside of bowl base.

With your loop still on your hook, insert your hook into the next st and through the corresponding st in the bowl top. Complete a sc. Repeat in remaining 23 sts. Fasten off and weave in ends.

Water

Note: When instructed to dec in this section, do *not* decrease normally (as outlined in Techniques). To dec, pull up a loop in next 2 sts so there are 3 loops on your hook. Yarn over and pull through all 3 loops.

Pick up the loop of Color B you dropped after finishing Rnd 7 of the bowl top. Continue:

Rnd 1: Dec 12 times—12 sts.

Rnd 2: Dec in all 6 sts—6 sts. Stuff lightly.

Fasten off with a sl st and use yarn needle to weave tail through the front loops of the remaining 6 sts, pulling tightly to close the hole. Weave in tail.

Food Bowl

Bowl Top

In Color C:

Rnd 1: Start 6 sc in an adjustable ring—6 sts.

Rnd 2: Inc 6 times—12 sts.

Rnd 3: (Sc 1, inc) 6 times—18 sts.

Rnd 4: Sc 1, inc, (sc 2, inc) 5 times, sc 1—24 sts.

Rnd 5: Sc in all 24 sts—24 sts.

Rnd 6: Sc in next 23 sts. In next st, change to Color D—24 sts.

Rnd 7: In FLO: sc in all 24 sts—24 sts.

Drop loop from hook and put a marker in it to save your place. Turn bowl inside out, with wrong side facing out.

Bowl Base

In Color A:

Rnd 1: Start 6 sc in an adjustable ring—6 sts.

Rnd 2: Inc 6 times—12 sts.

Rnd 3: (Sc 1, inc) 6 times—18 sts.

Rnd 4: Sc 1, inc, (sc 2, inc) 5 times, sc 1—24 sts.

Rnd 5: (Sc 5, inc) 4 times—28 sts.

Rnd 6: In BLO: sc in all 28 sts—28 sts.

Rnd 7: Sc 6, dec, sc 12, dec, sc 6—26 sts.

Rnd 8: (Sc 11, dec) 2 times—24 sts.

Do not fasten off. Place bowl top inside of bowl base.

With your loop still on your hook, insert your hook into the next st and through the corresponding leftover front loop of Color B. Complete a sc. Repeat in remaining 23 sts. Fasten off and weave in ends.

Food

Note: When instructed to dec in this section, do *not* decrease normally (as outlined in Techniques). To dec, pull up a loop in next 2 sts so there are 3 loops on your hook. Yarn over and pull through 2 loops, then yarn over and pull through remaining 2 loops. This method both decreases and also gives a bumpy texture that looks like kibble.

Pick up the loop of Color D you dropped after finishing Rnd 7 of the bowl top. Continue:

Rnd 1: (Sc 2, dec) 6 times—18 sts.

Rnd 2: (Sc 1, dec) 6 times—12 sts. Begin stuffing firmly.

Rnd 3: Dec in all sts—6 sts.

Fasten off with a sl st and use yarn needle to weave tail through the front loops of the remaining 6 sts, pulling tightly to close the hole. Weave in tail.

blossom

Breed: Pug

If there's something you need to get off your chest, Blossom is your go-to pup. With her superb listening skills, ability to maintain intense eye contact, and her calming, nonjudgmental aura, she's the doggy psychotherapist you didn't know you needed. Her hourly rates are very reasonable, and she accepts roast beef as payment.

FINISHED SIZE: 2in/5cm tall

SKILL LEVEL: Easy

MATERIALS

- Lion Brand® Vanna's Choice® 3.5oz/100g, 170yds/156m (100% acrylic)—one skein each: #860-125 Taupe (Color A), #860-123 Beige (Color B)
- Size D-3 (3.25mm) crochet hook
- Yarn needle
- Embroidery needle
- Black embroidery floss (for eyes and nose)
- Polyester stuffing
- Wooden stuffing stick
- Stitch markers and pins

Head and Body

In Color A:

Rnd 1: Ch 3. Starting in second ch from hook, sc 1. In next st, sc 4. On opposite side of foundation ch, sc 4 into next st—9 sts.

Rnd 2: Sc 2, inc, sc 3 into next st, sc 3, sc 3 into next st, inc—15 sts.

Rnd 3: Sc in all 15 sts, changing to Color B at end of rnd—15 sts.

Rnd 4: Sl st in all 15 sts—15 sts. Make sure to work each sl st loosely so you can work into them more easily in the next rounds.

Rnd 5: Sl st 5, sc 9, sc 3 into last st—17 sts.

Rnd 6: (Sc 3 into next st) 5 times, sc 12—27 sts.

Rnds 7–10: Sc in all 27 sts—27 sts. Embroider nose and eyes.

Rnd 11: Sc 3, inc, sc 6, inc, sc 7, inc, sc 8—30 sts.

Rnds 12–16: Sc in all 30 sts—30 sts.

Rnd 17: Sc 4, dec, (sc 8, dec) 2 times, sc 4—27 sts.

Rnd 18: (Sc 7, dec) 3 times—24 sts.

Begin stuffing the body, continuing to stuff firmly as you finish the following rounds.

Rnd 19: Sc 1, dec, (sc 2, dec) 5 times, sc 1—18 sts.

Rnd 20: (Sc 1, dec) 6 times—12 sts.

Rnd 21: Dec 6 times—6 sts.

Fasten off with a sl st, leaving a tail. Using a yarn needle, thread the tail through each of the front loops of the remaining 6 sts, pulling tightly to close hole. Weave in and trim yarn.

Ears (Make 2)

In Color A:

Rnd 1: Start 5 sc in an adjustable ring—5 sts.

Rnd 2: Sc 1, inc, sc 3—6 sts.

Rnd 3: Sc in all 6 sts—6 sts.

Do not fasten off or stuff; remove marker, press flat, and insert hook through both sides to close top with 2 sc. Yarn over and pull through to fasten off, leaving a tail for sewing.

Feet (Make 4)

In Color B:

Rnd 1: Start 5 sc in an adjustable ring—5 sts.

Rnd 2: Sc in all 5 sts—5 sts.

Fasten off with a sl st, leaving a tail for assembly. Do not stuff.

Tail

In Color B:

Row 1: Ch 6, making sure to leave a long tail (8in) while making your slipknot.

Row 2: Starting in second ch from hook, hdc 5 in each st to create tail curl.

Yarn over and pull through to fasten off, leaving a tail for sewing.

ASSEMBLY

Parts can be assembled in whichever order you choose, as shown.

dog & bed

Bonus Pattern!

FINISHED SIZE: 4¾in/12cm by 3¾in/8.5cm by 1½in/4cm

SKILL LEVEL: Intermediate

MATERIALS

- Lion Brand® Vanna's Choice® 3.5oz/100g, 170yds/156m (100% acrylic)—one skein each: #860-130 Honey (Color A), #860-123 Beige (Color B)
- Size D-3 (3.25mm) crochet hook
- Yarn needle
- Pins

Bed Edge

In Color A:

Rnd 1: Ch 56. Starting in second ch from hook, sc 54. In next st, sc 4. On opposite side of foundation ch, sc 53. Sc 4 into next st—115 sts.

Rnds 2–8: Sc in all 115 sts—115 sts.

Do not fasten off or stuff; press flat and close bottom by single crocheting through both sides. Yarn over and pull through to fasten off, leaving an extra long tail (about 24in) for sewing.

Bed Bottom (Make 2, then join)

In Color A:

Rnd 1: Ch 4. Starting in 2nd ch from hook, sc in next 2 sts. Sc 4 into next st. On opposite side of foundation ch, sc 1. Sc 4 into next st—11 sts.

Rnd 2: Sc 3, sc 3 into next st, inc, sc 4, inc, sc 3 into next st—17 sts.

Rnd 3: Sc 4, inc in next 3 sts, sc 6, inc in next 3 sts, sc 1—23 sts.

Rnd 4: Sc 5, (inc, sc 1) 3 times, sc 6, (inc, sc 1) 3 times—29 sts.

.

Rnd 5: Sc 6, (inc, sc 2) 3 times, sc 5, (inc, sc 2) 3 times—35 sts.

Rnd 6: Sc 7, (inc, sc 3) 3 times, sc 5, (inc, sc 3) 2 times, inc, sc 2—41 sts.

Rnd 7: Sc 7, (inc, sc 4) 3 times, sc 5, (inc, sc 4) 2 times, inc, sc 3—47 sts.

Rnd 8: Sc 8, (inc, sc 5) 3 times, sc 5, (inc, sc 5) 2 times, inc, sc 3—53 sts.

Rnd 9: Sc 8, (inc, sc 6) 3 times, sc 5, (inc, sc 6) 2 times, inc, sc 4—59 sts.

Rnd 10: Sc 9, (inc, sc 7) 3 times, sc 5, (inc, sc 7) 2 times, inc, sc 4—65 sts.

Rnd 11: Sc 9, (inc, sc 8) 3 times, sc 5, (inc, sc 8) 2 times, inc, sc 5—71 sts.

When you finish the first bottom, fasten off and weave in tail. When you finish the second, do not fasten off. Sandwich the two bottoms together, wrong sides facing each other, and insert your hook through both layers, as shown. Sl st all the way around, then fasten off and weave in tail.

Bed Cushion

In Color B:

Rnd 1: Ch 4. Starting in 2nd ch from hook, sc in next 2 sts. Sc 4 into next st. On opposite side of foundation chain, sc 1. Sc 4 into next st—11 sts.

Rnd 2: Sc 3, sc 3 into next st, inc, sc 4, inc, sc 3 into next st—17 sts.

Rnd 3: Sc 4, inc in next 3 sts, sc 6, inc in next 3 sts, sc 1—23 sts.

Rnd 4: Sc 5, (inc, sc 1) 3 times, sc 6, (inc, sc 1) 3 times—29 sts.

Rnd 5: Sc 6, (inc, sc 2) 3 times, sc 5, (inc, sc 2) 3 times—35 sts.

Rnd 6: Sc 7, (inc, sc 3) 3 times, sc 5, (inc, sc 3) 2 times, inc, sc 2—41 sts.

Rnd 7: Sc 7, (inc, sc 4) 3 times, sc 5, (inc, sc 4) 2 times, inc, sc 3—47 sts.

Rnd 8: Sc 8, (inc, sc 5) 3 times, sc 5, (inc, sc 5) 2 times, inc, sc 3—53 sts.

Rnd 9: Sc 8, (inc, sc 6) 3 times, sc 5, (inc, sc 6) 2 times, inc, sc 4—59 sts.

Rnd 10: Sc 9, (inc, sc 7) 3 times, sc 5, (inc, sc 7) 2 times, inc, sc 4—65 sts.

Rnd 11: In BLO: sc in all 65 sts—65 sts.

Rnd 12: Sc in all 65 sts—65 sts.

Rnd 13: In BLO: sc 9, (dec, sc 7) 3 times, sc 5, (dec, sc 7) 2 times, dec, sc 4—59 sts.

Rnd 14: Sc 8, (dec, sc 6) 3 times, sc 5, (dec, sc 6) 2 times, dec, sc 4—53 sts.

Rnd 15: Sc 8, (dec, sc 5) 3 times, sc 5, (dec, sc 5) 2 times, dec, sc 3—47 sts.

Rnd 16: Sc 7, (dec, sc 4) 3 times, sc 5, (dec, sc 4) 2 times, dec, sc 3—41 sts.

Rnd 17: Sc 7, (dec, sc 3) 3 times, sc 5, (dec, sc 3) 2 times, dec, sc 2—35 sts.

Rnd 18: Sc 6, (dec, sc 2) 3 times, sc 5, (dec, sc 2) 3 times—29 sts.

Rnd 19: Dec 14 times, sc 1—15 sts.

Rnd 20: Dec 7 times, sc 1—8 sts.

Do not stuff. Fasten off with a sl st and use yarn needle to weave tail through the front loops of the remaining 8 sts, pulling tightly to close the hole. Weave in tail.

ASSEMBLY

Thread the leftover tail from the bed edge onto a yarn needle. Line the edge of the bed up along the bottom of the bed, as shown, leaving an opening of about 14 sts. Using the leftover yarn tail, whip-stitch the two pieces together as shown.

When the pieces are securely joined, weave in your yarn tail.

decker

Breed: Bernese Mountain Dog

Although his ancestors hail from the Swiss Alps, Decker is from a region in the north of Spain known for its mountains and its delicious cuisine. Even though "no" is the same in both Spanish and English, Decker doesn't seem to understand the word either way, and nothing seems to deter him from eating human food straight off the table. At least he manages to burn off all those calories by hiking.

FINISHED SIZE: 4¼in/10.75cm tall

SKILL LEVEL: Intermediate

MATERIALS

- Lion Brand® Vanna's Choice® 3.5oz/100g, 170yds/156m (100% acrylic)—one skein each: #860-153 Black (Color A), #860-100 White (Color B), #860-124 Toffee (Color C)
- Size D-3 (3.25mm) crochet hook
- Yarn needle
- Embroidery needle
- Gray or brown embroidery floss (for eyes)
- Polyester stuffing
- Wooden stuffing stick
- Stitch markers and pins

Muzzle

In Color B:

Rnd 1: Ch 3. Starting in second ch from hook, sc 1. In next st, sc 4. On opposite side of foundation ch, sc 4 into next st—9 sts.

Rnd 2: Sc 2, inc, sc 3 into next st, sc 3, sc 3 into next st, inc—15 sts.

Rnds 3–4: Sc in all 15 sts—15 sts.

Fasten off with a sl st, leaving a tail for assembly. Embroider nose.

Head and Body

Head and body are started in Color A. **Sections shown in purple** *are completed in Color B, and* sections shown in blue *are completed in Color C. See "Changing Colors" in the Techniques section for more information on how to change yarn colors.*

In Color A, except where noted:

Rnd 1: Ch 5. Starting in second ch from hook, sc 3. In next st, sc 4. On opposite side of foundation ch, sc 2. Sc 4 into next st—13 sts.

Rnd 2: Sc 4, sc 3 into next st, inc, sc 5, inc, sc 3 into next st—19 sts.

Rnd 3: Sc 5, inc in next 3 sts, sc 7, inc in next 3 sts, sc 1—25 sts.

Rnd 4: Sc 6, (inc, sc 1) 3 times, sc 1, **sc 4**, sc 2, (inc, sc 1) 3 times—31 sts.

Rnd 5: Sc 16, **sc 4**, sc 11—31 sts.

Rnds 6–7: Sc 13, sc 2, sc 1, **sc 4**, sc 1, sc 2, sc 8—31 sts.

Rnd 8: Sc 16, **sc 4**, sc 11—31 sts.

Rnd 9: Sc 10, inc, sc 5, **sc 4**, sc 5, inc, sc 5—33 sts.

Rnd 10: Sc 17, **sc 4**, sc 12—33 sts.

Rnds 11–12: Sc 14, **sc 12**, sc 7—33 sts.

Rnd 13: Sc 3, inc, sc 10, **sc 12**, sc 7—34 sts.

Rnd 14: Sc 12, inc, sc 2, **sc 12**, sc 2, inc, sc 4—36 sts. Embroider eyes.

Rnd 15: Sc 16, **sc 12**, sc 8—36 sts.

Rnd 16: Sc 16, **sc 11, inc**, sc 8—37 sts.

Rnd 17: Sc 16, **sc 13**, sc 8—37 sts.

Rnd 18: Sc 5, inc, sc 10, **sc 12, inc,** sc 8—39 sts.

Rnd 19: Sc 17, **sc 14**, sc 8—39 sts.

Rnd 20: Sc 15, inc, sc 1, **sc 13, inc,** sc 8—41 sts.

Rnd 21: Sc 18, **sc 15,** sc 8—41 sts.

Rnd 22: Sc 7, inc, sc 8, inc, **sc 14, inc,** sc 9—44 sts.

Rnd 23: Sc 20, **sc 16,** sc 8—44 sts.

Rnd 24: Sc 8, inc, sc 11, **sc 15, inc,** sc 8—46 sts.

Rnd 25: Sc 21, **sc 17,** sc 8—46 sts.

Rnd 26: Sc 19, inc, sc 1, **sc 16, inc,** sc 8—48 sts.

Remainder of rnds are worked in Color A only:

Rnd 27: Sc in all 48 sts—48 sts.

Rnd 28: Sc 3, dec, (sc 6, dec) 5 times, sc 3—42 sts.

Rnd 29: (Sc 5, dec) 6 times—36 sts.

Rnd 30: Sc 2, dec, (sc 4, dec) 5 times, sc 2—30 sts.

Rnd 31: (Sc 3, dec) 6 times—24 sts. Begin stuffing the body, continuing to stuff firmly as you finish the following rounds.

Rnd 32: Sc 1, dec, (sc 2, dec) 5 times, sc 1—18 sts.

Rnd 33: (Sc 1, dec) 6 times—12 sts.

Rnd 34: Dec 6 times—6 sts.

Fasten off with a sl st, leaving a tail. Using a yarn needle, thread the tail through each of the front loops of the remaining 6 sts, pulling tightly to close hole. Weave in and trim yarn.

Ears (Make 2)

In Color A:

Rnd 1: Start 7 sc in an adjustable ring—7 sts.

Rnd 2: Inc 7 times—14 sts.

Rnd 3: Sc in all 14 sts—14 sts.

Rnd 4: (Sc 5, dec) 2 times—12 sts.

Rnd 5: Sc in all 12 sts—12 sts.

Rnd 6: (Sc 4, dec) 2 times—10 sts.

Rnd 7: Sc in all 10 sts—10 sts.

Rnd 8: (Sc 3, dec) 2 times—8 sts.

Do not fasten off or stuff; remove marker, press flat and insert hook through both sides to close top with 3 sc. Yarn over and pull through to fasten off, leaving a tail for sewing.

Front Legs (Make 2)

In Color B:

Rnd 1: Start 6 sc in an adjustable ring—6 sts.

Rnd 2: (Sc 2, inc) 2 times—8 sts. Change to Color C.

Rnds 3–4: Sc in all 8 sts—8 sts. Change to Color A.

Rnd 5: Sc in all 8 sts—8 sts.

Do not fasten off or stuff; remove marker, press flat and insert hook through both sides to close top with 3 sc.

Yarn over and pull through to fasten off, leaving a tail for sewing.

Back Legs (Make 2)

In Color B:

Rnd 1: Start 7 sc in an adjustable ring—7 sts.

Rnd 2: Sc 3, inc, sc 2, inc—9 sts. Change to Color C.

Rnds 3–4: Sc in all 9 sts—9 sts. At end of Rnd 4, change to Color A.

Rnds 5–6: Sc in all 9 sts—9 sts.

Yarn over and pull through to fasten off, leaving a tail for sewing.

Tail (Make 2, then join)

In Color A:

Row 1: Ch 10, making sure to leave a long tail (8in) while making your slipknot.

Row 2: Starting in second ch from hook, hdc 2, dc 2 times in next 7 sts.

Yarn over and pull through to fasten off, leaving a tail for sewing. Sandwich the two tail pieces together so the sts are aligned, as shown, and use one of the remaining tails to whipstitch the pieces together, down both sides. Weave in and trim remaining tails, leaving one for assembly later.

ASSEMBLY

Parts can be assembled in whichever order you choose. Lightly stuff muzzle and back legs before assembly. Place muzzle, ears, and legs as shown.

saatchi

Breed: Shiba Inu

True to the characteristics of his breed, Saatchi has energy and brains to spare. Luckily for us, Saatchi chooses to channel his abilities into nondestructive activities. Saatchi loves reading about art history and politics, and he dreams of running for office one day. (If only Lincoln would help him set up a campaign website!)

FINISHED SIZE: 4½in/11.5cm tall

SKILL LEVEL: Easy

MATERIALS

- Lion Brand® Vanna's Choice® 3.5oz/100g, 170yds/156m (100% acrylic)—one skein each: #860-130 Honey (Color A), #860-123 Beige (Color B)
- Size D-3 (3.25mm) crochet hook
- Yarn needle
- Embroidery needle
- Black embroidery floss (for eyes and nose)
- Polyester stuffing
- Wooden stuffing stick
- Stitch markers and pins

Muzzle

*Muzzle is started in Color B. **Sections shown in purple** are completed in Color A. See "Changing Colors" in the Techniques section for more information on how to change yarn colors.*

In Color B, except where noted:

Rnd 1: Ch 3. Starting in second ch from hook, sc 1. In next st, sc 4. On opposite side of foundation ch, sc 4 into next st—9 sts.

Rnd 2: Sc 4, **sc 3**, sc 2—9 sts.

Rnd 3: Sc 4, **sc 4**, sc 1—9 sts.

Fasten off with a sl st, leaving a tail for assembly. Embroider nose.

Head and Body

*Head and body are started in Color A. **Sections shown in blue** are completed in Color B.*

In Color A, except where noted:

Rnd 1: Ch 4. Starting in second ch from hook, sc 2, sc 4 into next st. On other side of foundation ch, sc 1, sc 4 into next st—11 sts.

Rnd 2: Sc 3, sc 3 into next st, inc, sc 4, inc, sc 3 into next st—17 sts.

Rnd 3: Sc 4, inc, (sc 3, inc) 3 times—21 sts.

Rnd 4: Sc 3, inc, (sc 6, inc) 2 times, sc 3—24 sts.

Rnd 5: (Sc 7, inc) 3 times—27 sts.

Rnd 6: Sc 12, **sc 2**, sc 3, **sc 2**, sc 8—27 sts.

Rnd 7: Sc in all 27 sts—27 sts.

Rnd 8: Sc 9, inc, sc 12, inc, sc 4—29 sts.

Rnds 9–11: Sc 13, **sc 8 in FLO,** sc 8—29 sts.

Note: Color B sections are worked in FLO to lessen the appearance of the "tilt" as rounds are worked downward. Color B sections will still appear slightly biased to one side, but not as dramatically as they would if the sts were worked in both loops.

Rnd 12: Sc 4, ch 8. Starting in second ch from hook, place a new marker and sc 7 back down to base of ch. The new marker will now be the beginning of your rounds. Remove your original marker. When you reach the base of the ch, sc 9, **sc 8 in FLO**, sc 18, working your way back up the other side of the ch, sc 4 into the last st before marker—46 sts.

Rnd 13: (Inc, sc 2) 3 times, sc 7, **sc 8 in FLO**, sc 12, (inc, sc 2) 3 times, sc 1—52 sts.

Rnds 14–17: Sc 19, **sc 8 in FLO**, sc 25—52 sts.

Rnd 18: Sc 11, dec, sc 7, **sc 4, dec, sc 1 in FLO,** sc 10, dec, sc 11, dec—48 sts.

Rnd 19: Sc 3, dec, sc 6, dec, sc 5, **sc 1, dec, sc 4 in FLO,** sc 2, dec, (sc 6, dec) 2 times, sc 3—42 sts.

Rnd 20: Sc 11, dec, sc 3, **(dec, sc 1) 2 times in FLO,** sc 1, dec, (sc 2, dec) 2 times, sc 9—36 sts.

Rnd 21: Sc 10, dec, sc 1, dec, **sc 1, dec, sc 1 in FLO,** dec, (sc 1, dec) 2 times, sc 9—30 sts. Change to Color B.

Rnd 22: Sc 8, dec 6 times, sc 4, dec 3 times— 21 sts.

Note: The body may have an odd shape before stuffing; don't worry, this is normal! Begin stuffing the head and body, continuing to stuff firmly as you finish the following rounds, using your wooden stuffing stick to push stuffing into areas that need shaping.

Rnd 23: Dec 3 times, (sc 1, dec) 5 times—13 sts.

Rnd 24: Sc 1, dec 6 times — 7 sts.

Fasten off with a sl st, leaving a tail. Using a yarn needle, thread the tail through each of the front loops of the remaining 7 sts, pulling tightly to close hole. Weave in and trim yarn.

Legs (Make 4)

In Color A:

Rnd 1: Start 6 sc in an adjustable ring—6 sts.

Rnds 2–5: Sc in all 6 sts—6 sts.

Do not fasten off or stuff; remove marker, press flat and close top with 2 sc as shown.

Yarn over and pull through to fasten off, leaving a tail for sewing.

Ears (Make 2)

In Color A:

Rnd 1: Start 5 sc in an adjustable ring—5 sts.

Rnd 2: Sc 1, inc, sc 3—6 sts.

Rnd 3: (Sc 2, inc) 2 times—8 sts.

Rnd 4: (Sc 3, inc) 2 times—10 sts.

Rnd 5: Sc in all 10 sts—10 sts.

Fasten off with a sl st, leaving a tail for assembly. Do not stuff; press flat.

Tail (Make 2, then join)

Make one in Color A and one in Color B:

Row 1: Ch 12, making sure to leave a long tail (8in) while making your slipknot.

Row 2: Starting in fourth ch from hook, (dc 4 into each st) 5 times, dc 4.

ASSEMBLY

Parts can be assembled in whichever order you choose, as shown.

Yarn over and pull through to fasten off, leaving a tail for sewing. Sandwich the two tail pieces together so the sts are aligned, as shown, and use one of the remaining tails of Color A to whipstitch the pieces together, down both sides. Weave in and trim remaining tails, leaving one for assembly later.

wendy

Breed: Boston Terrier

Be careful around Wendy—she bites. It's not her fault, though! She wouldn't actually hurt a fly, but she watches so many horror movies that she's constantly on edge. The other pups have suggested that she cut back on her habit, but she can't seem to pull herself away from the television. Wendy is usually camped out in the living room with a bowl of popcorn inside her blanket fort— just don't sneak up behind her or make any loud noises.

FINISHED SIZE: 4¼in/10.75cm tall

SKILL LEVEL: Intermediate

MATERIALS

- Lion Brand® Vanna's Choice® 3.5oz/100g, 170yds/156m (100% acrylic)—one skein each: #860-153 Black (Color A), #860-100 White (Color B)
- Size D-3 (3.25mm) crochet hook
- Yarn needle
- Embroidery needle
- Black embroidery floss (for nose)
- White embroidery floss (for eyes)
- Polyester stuffing
- Wooden stuffing stick
- Stitch markers and pins

Muzzle

In Color B:

Rnd 1: Ch 3. Starting in second ch from hook, sc 1. In next st, sc 4. On opposite side of foundation ch, sc 4 into next st—9 sts.

Rnd 2: Sc 2, sc 3 into next st, inc, sc 3, inc, sc 3 into next st—15 sts.

Rnd 3: Sc in all 15 sts—15 sts.

Fasten off with a sl st, leaving a tail for assembly. Embroider nose.

Head

Head is started in Color A. Sections shown in blue are worked in Color B. See "Changing Colors" in the Techniques section for more information on how to change yarn colors.

In Color A, except where noted:

Rnd 1: Ch 4. Starting in second ch from hook, sc 2. Sc 4 into next st. On opposite side of foundation ch, sc 1. Sc 4 into next st—11 sts.

Rnd 2: Sc 3, sc 3 into next st, inc, sc 4, inc, sc 3 into next st—17 sts.

Rnd 3: Sc 4, inc 3 times, sc 1, **sc 2,** sc 2, inc 3 times, sc 2—23 sts.

Rnd 4: Sc 7, inc, sc 4, **sc 3,** inc, sc 6, inc—26 sts.

Rnd 5: Sc 13, **sc 2, inc,** sc 10—27 sts.

Rnd 6: Sc 2, inc, sc 10, **sc 5,** sc 9—28 sts.

Rnd 7: Sc 3, inc, sc 6, inc, sc 5, inc, sc 7, inc, sc 3—32 sts.

Rnds 8–10: Sc in all 32 sts—32 sts.

Rnd 11: Change to Color B in first st. Remainder of rnds are worked in Color B.

(Sc 14, dec) 2 times—30 sts. Embroider eyes, temporarily pinning muzzle to head as a guide.

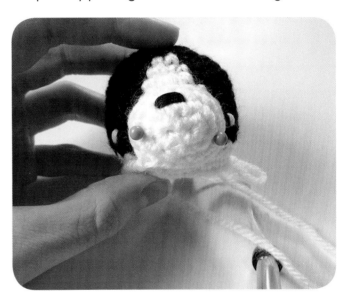

Rnd 12: (Sc 3, dec) 6 times—24 sts.

Rnd 13: Sc 1, dec, (sc 2, dec) 5 times, sc 1—18 sts.

Rnd 14: (Sc 1, dec) 6 times—12 sts.

Rnd 15: Dec 6 times—6 sts.

Fasten off with a sl st, leaving a tail. Using a yarn needle, thread the tail through each of the front loops of the remaining 6 sts, pulling tightly to close hole. Bring yarn out through bottom of head, leaving tail for assembly.

Body

Body is started in Color A. Sections bolded in blue are worked in Color B. See "Changing Colors" in the Techniques section for more information on how to change yarn colors.

In Color A, except where noted:

Rnd 1: Start 6 sc in an adjustable ring—6 sts.

Rnd 2: Inc 6 times—12 sts.

Rnd 3: (Sc 1, inc) 6 times—18 sts.

Rnd 4: Sc 1, inc, (sc 2, inc) 5 times, sc 1—24 sts.

Rnd 5: Sc 5, dec, sc 10, dec, sc 5—22 sts.

Rnd 6: Sc 1, **(inc, sc 1) 3 times,** sc 3, (dec, sc 1) 3 times, sc 3—22 sts.

Rnd 7: Sc 1, **sc 3, dec, sc 4,** sc 5, dec, sc 5—20 sts.

Rnd 8: Sc 1, **dec, sc 4, dec,** sc 5, dec, sc 4—17 sts.

Rnd 9: Sc 1, **sc 3, inc, sc 2,** sc 4, dec, sc 4—17 sts.

Rnd 10: Sc 1, **sc 3, dec, sc 2,** sc 4, dec, sc 3—15 sts.

Rnd 11: Sc 1, **sc 2, dec, sc 2,** sc 3, dec, sc 3—13 sts.

Fasten off with a sl st, weaving in tail. Stuff lightly.

Ears (Make 2)

In Color A:

Rnd 1: Start 5 sc in an adjustable ring—5 sts.

Rnd 2: Sc 1, inc, sc 3—6 sts.

Rnd 3: (Sc 2, inc) 2 times—8 sts.

Rnd 4: (Sc 3, inc) 2 times—10 sts.

Rnd 5: (Sc 4, inc) 2 times—12 sts.

Rnd 6: (Sc 5, inc) 2 times—14 sts.

Rnd 7: Sc 3, inc, sc 6, inc, sc 3—16 sts.

Rnd 8: (Sc 7, inc) 2 times—18 sts.

Rnd 9: Sc 4, inc, sc 8, inc, sc 4—20 sts.

Fasten off with a sl st, leaving a tail for assembly. Do not stuff. Press flat and pinch sides of ear together to give ear its shape.

Front Legs (Make 2)

In Color B:

Rnd 1: Start 5 sc in an adjustable ring—5 sts.

Rnds 2–4: Sc in all 5 sts—5 sts.

Do not fasten off or stuff; remove marker, press flat and insert hook through both sides to close top with 2 sc. Yarn over and pull through to fasten off, leaving a tail for sewing.

Back Legs (Make 2)

In Color A:

Rnd 1: Start 5 sc in an adjustable ring—5 sts.

Rnds 2–3: Sc in all 5 sts—5 sts.

Do not fasten off or stuff; remove marker, press flat and insert hook through both sides to close top with 2 sc. Yarn over and pull through to fasten off, leaving a tail for sewing.

ASSEMBLY

Sew muzzle to head.

Sew head to body using leftover yarn tail from head, as shown, adding more stuffing to body as you go.

After head is attached to body, sew on the remainder of parts in whichever order you choose.

Victor

Breed: Bull Terrier

As a staunch minimalist and neat freak, Victor is always irritated by all of the *stuff* that the other pups seem to acquire and the mess they manage to make around the house. He is always tidying things and grumbling to himself: *Who brought all these sticks in from the yard? Why does anyone need seven tennis balls? Whose drool is this? Arghh!*

FINISHED SIZE: 4½in/11.5cm tall

SKILL LEVEL: Intermediate

MATERIALS

- Lion Brand® Vanna's Choice® 3.5oz/100g, 170yds/156m (100% acrylic)—one skein: #860-100 White
- Size D-3 (3.25mm) crochet hook
- Yarn needle
- Embroidery needle
- Black embroidery floss (for eyes and nose)
- Polyester stuffing
- Wooden stuffing stick
- Stitch markers and pins

Head

Rnd 1: Start 6 sc in an adjustable ring—6 sts.

Rnd 2: (Sc 1, inc) 3 times—9 sts.

Rnd 3: (Sc 3, inc) 3 times, sc 3—12 sts.

Rnd 4: Sc in all 12 sts—12 sts.

Rnd 5: Sc 3, (inc, sc 1) 3 times, sc 3—15 sts.

Rnd 6: Sc 3, (inc, sc 1) 4 times, sc 4—19 sts.

Rnd 7: Sc 4, (inc, sc 1) 5 times, sc 5—24 sts. Embroider nose.

Rnd 8: Sc 3, (inc, sc 2) 6 times, sc 3—30 sts.

Rnds 9–11: Sc in all 30 sts—30 sts.

Rnd 12: Sc 5, (dec, sc 2) 5 times, sc 5—25 sts. Embroider eyes.

Rnd 13: Dec, (sc 2, dec) 5 times, sc 3—19 sts. Begin stuffing the head, continuing to stuff firmly as you finish the following rounds.

Rnd 14: Sc 3, dec, (sc 2, dec) 3 times, sc 2— 15 sts.

Rnd 14: Dec 7 times, remove marker and dec— 6 sts.

Fasten off with a sl st, leaving a tail. Using a yarn needle, thread the tail through each of the front loops of the remaining 6 sts, pulling tightly to close hole. Weave in and trim yarn.

Body

Rnd 1: Ch 13, making sure to leave a long tail (at least 8 in) while making your slipknot. Insert hook into first ch and pull through a sl st to join the two ends of the chain.

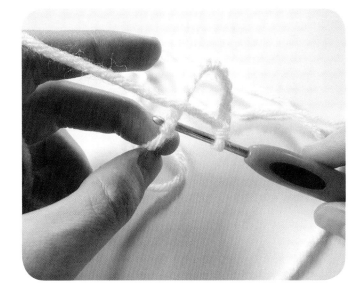

Rnd 2: Sc in all 13 sts—13 sts.

Rnd 3: Sc 1, ch 5. Starting in second ch from hook, place a new marker and sc 4 back down to base of ch. This will be the new beginning of your round. Remove your original marker. When you reach the base of the ch, continue working into the next sts in the round normally: sc 15, working your way back up the other side of the ch, sc 4 into last st before marker— 24 sts.

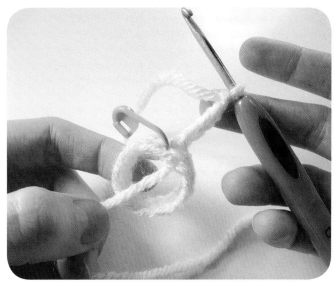

loops of the remaining 5 sts, pulling tightly to close hole. Weave in and trim yarn. Finish stuffing the body firmly through the neck.

Rnd 4: (Inc, sc 1) 2 times, sc 14, (inc, sc 1) 2 times, sc 1, inc—29 sts.

Rnd 5: Sc in all 29 sts—29 sts.

Rnd 6: Sc 28, inc—30 sts.

Rnd 7: Sc 12, inc, sc 17—31 sts.

Rnd 8: Sc in all 31 sts—31 sts.

Rnd 9: (Sc 2, dec) 2 times, sc 6, dec, sc 5, (dec, sc 2) 2 times, dec—25 sts.

Rnd 10: (Sc 3, dec) 5 times—20 sts.

Rnd 11: (Sc 2, dec) 5 times—15 sts. Stuff body lightly.

Rnd 12: (Sc 1, dec) 5 times—10 sts.

Rnd 13: Dec 5 times—5 sts.

Fasten off with a sl st, leaving a tail. Using a yarn needle, thread the tail through each of the front

Ears (Make 2)

Rnd 1: Start 5 sc in an adjustable ring—5 sts.

Rnd 2: Sc 1, inc, sc 3—6 sts.

Rnd 3: Sc 4, inc, sc 1—7 sts.

Rnd 4: Sc in all 7 sts—7 sts.

Rnd 5: Inc, sc 3, inc, sc 2—9 sts

Rnd 6: Sc in all 9 sts—9 sts.

Rnd 7: Inc, sc 3, inc, sc 4—11 sts.

Do not fasten off or stuff; remove marker, press flat, and insert hook through both sides to close top with 5 sc. Yarn over and pull through to fasten off, leaving a tail for sewing.

Front Legs (Make 2)

Rnd 1: Start 6 sc in an adjustable ring—6 sts.

Rnds 2–5: Sc in all 6 sts—6 sts.

Do not fasten off or stuff; remove marker, press flat, and insert hook through both sides to close top with 2 sc. Yarn over and pull through to fasten off, leaving a tail for sewing.

Back Legs (Make 2)

Rnd 1: Start 6 sc in an adjustable ring—6 sts.

Rnds 2–4: Sc in all 6 sts—6 sts.

Do not fasten off or stuff; remove marker, press flat and insert hook through both sides to close top with 2 sc. Yarn over and pull through to fasten off, leaving a tail for sewing.

Tail

Row 1: Ch 8, making sure to leave a long tail (8in) while making your slipknot.

Row 2: Starting in second ch from hook, sl st, sc 3, hdc 3.

Yarn over and pull through to fasten off, leaving a tail for sewing.

ASSEMBLY

Attach the head to the body as shown.

After head is attached to body, sew on the remainder of the parts in whichever order you choose.

cookie

Breed: Jack Russell Terrier

Don't let his cute name or his innocent baby face fool you: Cookie is a stone-cold bad boy. Around these parts, they call him the Jack Russell Terror, and for good reason. You can usually find him up on the roof barking at passersby (how did he get up there?) or out in the backyard setting off illegal fireworks that he got in the next state over (seriously, just how?). We've got a lot of questions for Cookie, but we're too afraid to ask.

FINISHED SIZE: 3½in/9cm tal

SKILL LEVEL: Intermediate

MATERIALS

- Lion Brand® Vanna's Choice® 3.5oz/100g, 170yds/156m (100% acrylic)—one skein each: #860-100 White (Color A), #860-124 Toffee (Color B)
- Size D-3 (3.25mm) crochet hook
- Yarn needle
- Embroidery needle
- Black embroidery floss (for eyes and nose)
- Polyester stuffing
- Wooden stuffing stick
- Stitch markers and pins

Muzzle and Head

Head and body are started in Color A. Sections shown in blue are worked in Color B. See "Changing Colors" in the Techniques section for more information on how to change yarn colors.

In Color A, except where noted:

Rnd 1: Ch 3. Starting in second ch from hook, sc 1. In next st, sc 4. On opposite side of foundation ch, sc 4 into next st—9 sts.

Rnds 2–3: Sc in all 9 sts—9 sts.

Rnd 4: (Sc 3 into next st) 2 times, sc 3 into next st, sc 6—15 sts.

Rnd 5: Sc 6, sc 3, inc, sc 2, inc, sc 2—17 sts.

Rnd 6: Inc, (sc 1, sc 3 into next st) 2 times, sc 1, sc 3 into next st, sc 2, sc 8—24 sts.

Rnds 7–10: Sc 11, sc 5, sc 8—24 sts. Embroider eyes and nose.

Rnd 11: (Sc 4, dec) 4 times—20 sts.

Rnd 12: (Sc 3, dec) 4 times—16 sts. Begin stuffing the head, continuing to stuff firmly as you finish the following rounds.

Rnd 13: (Sc 2, dec) 4 times—12 sts.

Rnd 14: Dec 6 times—6 sts.

Fasten off with a sl st, leaving a tail. Using a yarn needle, thread the tail through each of the front loops of the remaining 6 sts, pulling tightly to close hole. Weave in and trim yarn.

Body

Body is started in Color A. Sections shown in blue are completed in Color B. See "Changing Colors" in the Techniques section for more information on how to change yarn colors.

In Color A, except where noted:

Rnd 1: Ch 10, making sure to leave a long tail (at least 8 in) while making your slipknot. Insert hook into first ch and pull through a sl st to join the two ends of the chain.

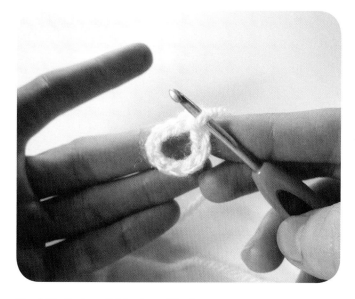

Rnd 2: Sc in all 10 sts—10 sts.

Rnd 3: Sc 1, ch 6. Starting in second ch from hook, place a new marker. This will be the new beginning of your round. Remove your original marker. Continue: (sc 1, inc) 2 times, sc 3, inc, sc 4, inc, sc 3, inc, sc 1, inc, sc 4 into last st before marker—29 sts.

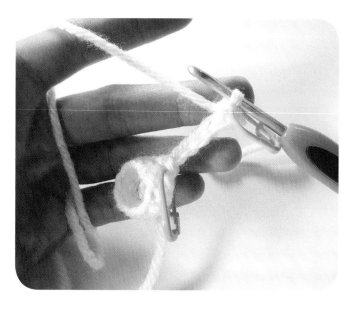

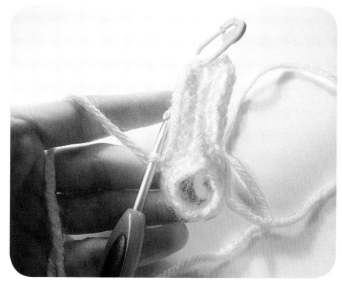

Rnd 4: Sc 19, sc 5, sc 4, inc—30 sts.

Rnds 5–7: Sc 19, sc 5, sc 6—30 sts.

Rnd 8: (Sc 2, dec) 2 times, sc 5, dec, sc 4, sc 1, dec, sc 2, dec, sc 2, dec—24 sts.

Rnd 9: Sc 3, dec, sc 2, dec, sc 1, dec, sc 3, dec, sc 2, dec, sc 1, dec—18 sts.

Rnd 10: (Sc 1, dec) 6 times—12 sts. Begin stuffing body lightly.

Rnd 11: Dec 6 times—6 sts.

Fasten off with a sl st, leaving a tail. Using a yarn needle, thread the tail through each of the front loops of the remaining 6 sts, pulling tightly to close hole. Weave in and trim yarn. Finish stuffing the body firmly through the neck.

Ears (Make 2)

Make one in Color A and one in Color B:

Rnd 1: Start 5 sc in an adjustable ring—5 sts.

Rnd 2: Sc 1, inc, sc 3—6 sts.

Rnd 3: (Sc 2, inc) 2 times—8 sts.

Rnd 4: Sc in all 8 sts—8 sts.

Do not fasten off or stuff; remove marker, press flat and insert hook through both sides to close top with 3 sc.

Yarn over and pull through to fasten off, leaving a tail for sewing.

Front Legs (Make 2)

In Color A:

Rnd 1: Start 5 sc in an adjustable ring—5 sts.

Rnds 2–5: Sc in all 5 sts—5 sts.

Do not fasten off or stuff; remove marker, press flat and insert hook through both sides to close top with 2 sc.

Yarn over and pull through to fasten off, leaving a tail for sewing.

Back Legs (Make 2)

In Color A:

Rnd 1: Start 5 sc in an adjustable ring—5 sts.

Rnds 2–3: Sc in all 5 sts—5 sts.

Do not fasten off or stuff; remove marker, press flat and insert hook through both sides to close top with 2 sc. Yarn over and pull through to fasten off, leaving a tail for sewing.

Tail

In Color A:

Row 1: Ch 6, making sure to leave a long tail (8in) while making your slipknot.

Row 2: Starting in second ch from hook, sl st, sc 4.

Yarn over and pull through to fasten off, leaving a tail for sewing.

ASSEMBLY

Attach the head to the body as shown.

After head is attached to body, sew on the remainder of the parts in whichever order you choose.

Pappy

Breed: Scottish Terrier

You wouldn't know it by looking at him, but Pappy is actually one of the younger pups in the house. With his long whiskers and eyebrows, he was once mistaken for a grandpa, and he just decided to fully embrace the look. He walks around with a novelty pipe, giving out butterscotch candies and telling stories about the war. Now that's dedication.

FINISHED SIZE: 3½in/9cm tall

SKILL LEVEL: Experienced

MATERIALS

- Lion Brand® Vanna's Choice® 3.5oz/100g, 170yds/156m (100% acrylic)—one skein: #860-151 Charcoal Gray
- Size D-3 (3.25mm) crochet hook
- Yarn needle
- Embroidery needle
- Black embroidery floss (for eyes and nose)
- Polyester stuffing
- Wooden stuffing stick
- Stitch markers and pins

Muzzle and Head

*While making the head, **sections shown in purple** are worked in FLO. In following rounds, work into the remaining back loops normally.*

Rnd 1: Ch 3. Starting in second ch from hook, sc 1. In next st, sc 4. On opposite side of foundation ch, sc 4 into next st—9 sts.

Rnd 2: Sc in all 9 sts—9 sts.

Rnd 3: Sc 2, **in next st: sc 1, ch 7, starting in second ch from hook, sl st 6 down ch, sl st in same st at base of ch**, sc 5, **in next st: sc 1, ch 7, starting in second ch from hook, sl st 6 down ch, sl st in same st at base of ch**—9 sts.

Rnd 4: Sc 3, inc, sc 4, inc—11 sts.

Rnd 5: Sc 3, **in next st: sc 1, ch 7, starting in second ch from hook, sl st 6 down ch, sl st in same st at base of ch**, sc 7—11 sts.

Rnd 6: **In first st: sc 1, ch 7, starting in second ch from hook, sl st 6 down ch, sl st in same st at base of ch**, sc 10—11 sts. Embroider nose.

Rnd 7: Sc 4, **in next st: sc 1, ch 8, starting in second ch from hook, sl st 7 down ch, sl st in same st at base of ch**, sc 6—11 sts.

Rnd 8: **In first st: sc 1, ch 7, starting in second ch from hook, sl st 6 down ch, sl st in same st at base of ch**, (sc 3 into next st) 4 times, sc 6—19 sts.

Rnd 9: Sc in all 19 sts—19 sts.

Rnd 10: Sc 1, inc, sc 3, sc 3 into next st, sc 2, sc 3 into next st, sc 4, inc, sc 5—25 sts. Embroider eyes.

Rnd 11: Sc 5, **(sc 1, ch 4, starting in second ch from hook, sl st 3 down ch, sl st in same st at base of ch) 2 times**, (sc 1, inc) 3 times, **(sc 1, ch 4, starting in second ch from hook, sl st 3 down ch, sl st in same st at base of ch) 2 times**, sc 10—28 sts.

Rnd 12: Sc in all 28 sts—28 sts.

Rnd 13: (Sc 5, dec) 4 times—24 sts.

Rnd 14: Sc 2, dec, (sc 4, dec) 3 times, sc 2—20 sts.

Rnd 15: Sc 4, dec, sc 3, dec, sc 4, dec, sc 3—17 sts. Begin stuffing the head, continuing to stuff firmly as you finish the following rounds.

Rnd 16: (Sc 3, dec) 3 times, sc 2—14 sts.

Rnd 17: Dec 7 times—7 sts.

Rnd 18: Dec, stop and do not complete rest of rnd—6 sts.

Fasten off with a sl st, leaving a tail. Using a yarn needle, thread the tail through each of the front loops of the remaining 6 sts, pulling tightly to close hole. Weave in and trim yarn.

Body

Rnd 1: Ch 10, making sure to leave a long tail (at least 8 in) while making your slipknot. Insert hook into first ch and pull through a sl st to join the two ends of the chain.

Rnd 2: Sc 1, ch 6. Starting in second ch from hook, place a new marker. This will be the new beginning of your round. Remove your original marker. Continue: (sc 1, inc) 2 times, sc 3, inc, sc 4, inc, sc 3, inc, sc 1, inc, sc 4 into last st before marker—29 sts.

Rnd 3: Sc 28, inc—30 sts.

Rnd 4: Sc in all 30 sts—30 sts. Continue to create outside fur:

Rnd 5a: In FLO: sc 7, inc, sc 14, inc, sc 7—32 sts.

Rnd 5b: (Sc 15, inc) 2 times—34 sts.

Rnd 5c: Sc 8, inc, sc 16, inc, sc 8—36 sts.

Rnd 5d: Sc in all 36 sts—36 sts.

Rnd 5e: In FLO: (sc 1, ch 2, sl st in same st) in each st around to create fringe at bottom of body.

Fasten off and weave in tail. Join a new piece of yarn where you left off at end of Rnd 4 and continue.

Rnd 5 (continued from end of Rnd 4): In leftover back loops of Rnd 4, sc in all 30 sts—30 sts.

Note: You may find it easiest to turn the outside fur upwards to work on the remaining rounds.

Rnd 6: Sc in all 30 sts—30 sts.

Rnd 7: (Sc 2, dec) 2 times, (sc 5, dec) 2 times, (sc 2, dec) 2 times—24 sts.

Rnd 8: (Sc 3, dec, sc 2, dec, sc 1, dec) 2 times—18 sts. Begin stuffing body lightly.

Rnd 9: (Sc 1, dec) 6 times—12 sts.

Rnd 10: Dec 6 times—6 sts.

Fasten off with a sl st, leaving a tail. Using a yarn needle, thread the tail through each of the front loops of the remaining 6 sts, pulling tightly to close hole. Weave in and trim yarn. Finish stuffing the body firmly through the neck.

Ears (Make 2)

Rnd 1: Start 5 sc in an adjustable ring—5 sts.

Rnd 2: Inc, sc 4—6 sts.

Rnd 3: (Sc 2, inc) 2 times—8 sts.

Do not fasten off or stuff; remove marker, press flat and close top with 3 sc as shown.

Yarn over and pull through to fasten off, leaving a tail for sewing.

Tail

Row 1: Ch 8, making sure to leave a long tail (8in) while making your slipknot.

Row 2: Starting in second ch from hook, sc 2, hdc 5.

Yarn over and pull through to fasten off, leaving a tail for sewing.

ASSEMBLY

Attach the head to the body as shown.

After head is attached to body, sew on the remainder of the parts in whichever order you choose.

Note: Pappy's whiskers can get pretty unruly, so if you'd like, you can use a dab or two of fabric glue to keep them in place!

boris

Breed: Husky

Elusive and mysterious, Boris is rarely around due to his demanding job outside of the house. What does he do for a living, and how did a dog even become employed in the first place? Nobody knows. Since he doesn't have to worry about living expenses or bills, Boris spends his hard-earned cash on extravagant trips overseas and lavish meals in Michelin Star restaurants.

FINISHED SIZE: 4½in/11.5cm tall

SKILL LEVEL: Experienced

MATERIALS

- Lion Brand® Vanna's Choice® 3.5oz/100g, 170yds/156m (100% acrylic)—one skein each: #860-149 Silver Gray (Color A), #860-100 White (Color B)
- Size D-3 (3.25mm) crochet hook
- Yarn needle
- Embroidery needle
- Black embroidery floss (for eyes and nose)
- Polyester stuffing
- Wooden stuffing stick
- Stitch markers and pins

Muzzle

In Color B:

Rnd 1: Ch 3. Starting in second ch from hook, sc 1. In next st, sc 4. On opposite side of foundation ch, sc 4 into next st—9 sts.

Rnds 2–3: Sc in all 9 sts—9 sts.

Fasten off with a sl st, leaving a tail for assembly. Embroider nose.

Head and Body

Head and body are started in Color A. Sections shown in blue are completed in Color B. See "Changing Colors" in the Techniques section for more information on how to change yarn colors.

In Color A, except where noted:

Rnd 1: Ch 4. Starting in second ch from hook, sc 2, sc 4 into next st. On opposite side of foundation ch, sc 1, sc 4 into next st—11 sts.

Rnd 2: Sc 3, sc 3 into next st, inc, sc 4, inc, sc 3 into next st—17 sts.

Rnd 3: Sc 4, inc, sc 2, sc 1, inc, sc 2, sc 1, sc 1, inc, sc 2, inc—21 sts.

Rnd 4: Sc 3, inc, sc 2, inc, sc 1, sc 2, sc 1, inc, sc 1, sc 2, sc 2, inc, sc 3—25 sts.

Rnd 5: Sc 8, inc, sc 1, sc 3, sc 3, sc 3, sc 2, inc, sc 3—27 sts.

Rnd 6: Sc 11, sc 4, sc 2, sc 4, sc 6—27 sts.

Rnds 7–8: Sc 11, sc 11, sc 5—27 sts.

Rnd 9: Sc 11, in FLO: sc 11, sc 5—27 sts.

Note: Color B sections are worked in FLO to lessen the appearance of the "tilt" as rounds are worked downward. Color B sections will still appear slightly biased to one side, but not as dramatically as they would if the sts were worked in both loops.

Rnd 10: Sc 11, in FLO: sc 10, inc, sc 5—28 sts.

Rnd 11: Sc 11, in FLO: sc 12, sc 5—28 sts. Embroider eyes.

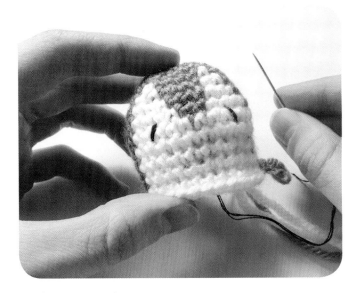

Rnd 12: Sc 4, ch 8.

Starting in second ch from hook, place a new marker. This will be the new beginning of your round. Remove your original marker. Continue: (inc, sc 2) 2 times, inc, sc 8, in FLO: sc 12, sc 11, (inc, sc 2) 2 times, sc 4 into last st before marker—52 sts.

Rnd 13: Sc 18, in FLO: sc 12, sc 21, inc—53 sts.

Rnds 14–15: Sc 18, in FLO: sc 12, sc 23—53 sts.

Rnd 16: Sc 18, in FLO: sc 12, sc 22, inc—54 sts.

Rnd 17: Sc 2, dec, sc 5, dec, sc 7, in FLO: (sc 2, dec) 3 times, sc 7, dec, sc 6, dec, sc 7—47 sts.

Rnd 18: Sc 16, in FLO: sc 9, sc 20, dec—46 sts.

Rnd 19: Sc 4, dec, sc 6, dec, sc 2, in FLO: dec, sc 2, dec, sc 1, dec, sc 2, dec, sc 6, dec, sc 9—39 sts.

Rnd 20: Sc 11, dec, sc 1, in FLO: (dec, sc 1) 2 times, sc 1, dec, sc 16—35 sts.

Rnd 21: Change to Color B in first st. Remainder of rnds are worked in Color B. (Sc 5, dec) 5 times—30 sts.

Note: The body may have an odd shape before stuffing; don't worry, this is normal!

Begin stuffing the head and body, continuing to stuff firmly as you finish the following rounds, using your wooden stuffing stick to push stuffing into areas that need shaping.

Rnd 22: (Sc 3, dec) 6 times—24 sts.

Rnd 23: Sc 1, dec, (sc 2, dec) 5 times, sc 1—18 sts.

Rnd 24: (Sc 1, dec) 6 times—12 sts.

Rnd 25: Dec 6 times—6 sts.

Fasten off with a sl st, leaving a tail. Using a yarn needle, thread the tail through each of the front loops of the remaining 6 sts, pulling tightly to close hole. Weave in and trim yarn.

Front Legs (Make 2)

In Color A:

Rnd 1: Start 6 sc in an adjustable ring—6 sts.

Rnds 2–7: Sc in all 6 sts—6 sts.

Do not fasten off or stuff; remove marker, press flat and insert hook through both sides to close top with 2 sc. Yarn over and pull through to fasten off, leaving a tail for sewing.

Back Legs (Make 2)

In Color A:

Rnd 1: Start 6 sc in an adjustable ring—6 sts.

Rnds 2–6: Sc in all 6 sts—6 sts.

Do not fasten off or stuff; remove marker, press flat and insert hook through both sides to close top with 2 sc. Yarn over and pull through to fasten off, leaving a tail for sewing.

Ears (Make 2)

In Color A:

Rnd 1: Start 5 sc in an adjustable ring—5 sts.

Rnd 2: Sc 1, inc, sc 3—6 sts.

Rnd 3: (Sc 2, inc) 2 times—8 sts.

Rnd 4: (Sc 3, inc) 2 times—10 sts.

Rnd 5: (Sc 4, inc) 2 times—12 sts.

Fasten off with a sl st, leaving a tail for assembly. Do not stuff; press flat.

Tail (Make 2, then join)

Make one in Color A and one in Color B:

Row 1: Ch 11, making sure to leave a long tail (8in) while making your slipknot.

Row 2: Starting in second ch from hook, sc, hdc 2 times in next st, dc 2 times in next 4 sts, dc 5.

Yarn over and pull through to fasten off, leaving a tail for sewing. Sandwich the two tail pieces together so the stitches are aligned, as shown, and use one of the remaining tails of Color A to whipstitch the pieces together, down both sides.

Weave in and trim remaining tails, leaving one for assembly later.

ASSEMBLY

Parts can be assembled in whichever order you choose, as shown.

malcolm

Breed: Standard Poodle

Often described as a "good sir" and a "very nice chap," chances are Malcolm is the first (and maybe even the friendliest) pup you'll encounter when entering the house. He loves greeting visitors and considers himself the official tour guide—he just loves his home and he's so proud to show it off!

FINISHED SIZE: 4in/10cm tall

SKILL LEVEL: Experienced

MATERIALS

- Lion Brand® Vanna's Choice® 3.5oz/100g, 170yds/156m (100% acrylic)—one skein: #860-098 Fisherman
- Size D-3 (3.25mm) crochet hook
- Yarn needle
- Embroidery needle
- Black embroidery floss (for eyes and nose)
- Polyester stuffing
- Wooden stuffing stick
- Stitch markers and pins

Head

*While making the head, **sections shown in purple** are worked in FLO. In following rounds, work into the remaining back loops normally.*

Rnd 1: Ch 3. Starting in second ch from hook, sc 1. In next st, sc 4. On opposite side of foundation ch, sc 4 into next st—9 sts.

Rnds 2–3: Sc in all 9 sts—9 sts.

Rnd 4: Sc 4, (sc 3 into next st) 4 times, sc 1—17 sts.

Rnd 5: Sc in all 17 sts—17 sts.

Rnd 6: Sc 5, (inc, sc 1) 6 times—23 sts. Embroider nose.

Rnd 7: Sc 11, (sc 3 into next st, sc 1) 3 times, sc 6—29 sts.

Rnd 8: Sc 15, **(in next st: sc 1, ch 3, sl st in same st) 5 times,** sc 9—29 sts.

Rnd 9: Sc in all 29 sts—29 sts.

Rnd 10: Sc 14, **(in next st: sc 1, ch 3, sl st in same st) 7 times,** sc 8—29 sts.

Rnd 11: Sc in all 29 sts—29 sts.

Rnd 12: Sc 8, dec, sc 3, **(in next st: sc 1, ch 3, sl st in same st) 7 times,** sc 4, dec, sc 3—27 sts.

Rnd 13: Sc in all 27 sts—27 sts. Embroider eyes.

Rnd 14: (Sc 3, dec) 2 times, sc 5, **(in next st: sc 1, ch 3, sl st in same st) 5 times,** sc 3, dec, sc 2—24 sts.

Rnd 15: Sc 2, dec, (sc 4, dec) 3 times, sc 2—20 sts.

Rnd 16: (Sc 3, dec) 2 times, sc 2, **(in next st: sc 1, ch 3, slst in same st) 2 times,** (sc 1, dec) 2 times—16 sts. Begin stuffing the head, continuing to stuff firmly as you finish the following rounds.

Rnd 17: (Sc 2, dec) 4 times—12 sts.

Rnd 18: Dec 6 times—6 sts.

Fasten off with a sl st, leaving a tail. Using a yarn needle, thread the tail through each of the front loops of the remaining 6 sts, pulling tightly to close hole. Weave in and trim yarn.

Body

Rnd 1: Ch 12, making sure to leave a long tail (at least 8 in) while making your slipknot. Insert hook into first ch and pull through a sl st to join the two ends of the chain.

Rnd 2: In same st, place marker and begin round. Sc in all 12 sts—12 sts.

Rnd 3: Sc 1, ch 8. Starting in second ch from hook, place a new marker. This will be the new beginning of your round. Remove your original marker. Continue: sc 1, inc, sc 2, inc, sc 16, inc, sc 2, inc, sc 4 into last st before marker—33 sts.

Rnd 4: Sc 12, inc, sc 5, inc, sc 14—35 sts.

Rnd 5: Sc 34, inc—36 sts.

Rnd 6: (Sc 3, dec) 2 times, sc 13, dec, sc 3, dec, sc 4, inc, sc 1—33 sts.

Rnd 7: Sc in all 33 sts—33 sts.

Rnd 8: Sc 30, dec, remove marker and dec, placing marker in completed dec—31 sts.

Rnd 9: Beginning in next st after marker (do not move marker, just keep working): sc 1, dec, sc 2, dec, sc 6, dec, sc 3, dec, (sc 2, dec) 2 times, sc 2—25 sts.

Rnd 10: (Sc 2, dec) 2 times, sc 4, dec, sc 3, dec, sc 2, dec, sc 2—20 sts. Begin stuffing body lightly.

Rnd 11: (Sc 1, dec) 2 times, sc 3, dec, sc 2, dec, sc 1, dec 2 times—14 sts.

Rnd 12: Dec 7 times—7 sts.

Rnd 13: Dec, stop and do not continue rnd—6 sts.

Fasten off with a sl st, leaving a tail. Using a yarn needle, thread the tail through each of the front loops of the remaining 6 sts, pulling tightly to close hole. Weave in and trim yarn. Finish stuffing the body firmly through the neck.

Ears (Make 2)

Rnd 1: Start 6 sc in an adjustable ring—6 sts.

Rnd 2: In FLO: (sc 1, ch 3, sl st in same st) 6 times.

Rnd 3: In back loops remaining from Rnd 2: inc 6 times—12 sts.

Rnd 4: In FLO: (sc 1, ch 3, sl st in same st) 12 times.

Rnd 5: In back loops remaining from Rnd 4: sc in all 12 sts—12 sts.

Rnd 6: (Sc 4, dec) 2 times—10 sts.

Rnd 7: (Sc 3, dec) 2 times—8 sts.

Rnd 8: Sc in all 8 sts—8 sts.

Do not fasten off or stuff; remove marker, press flat and close top with 3 sc.

Yarn over and pull through to fasten off, leaving a tail for sewing.

Front Legs (Make 2)

Rnd 1: Start 6 sc in an adjustable ring—6 sts.

Rnds 2–3: Sc in all 6 sts—6 sts.

Rnd 4: In FLO: (sc 1, ch 3, sl st in same st) 6 times.

Rnd 5: In back loops remaining from Rnd 2: sc in all 6 sts—6 sts.

Rnds 6–8: Sc in all 6 sts.

Do not fasten off or stuff; remove marker, press flat and close top with 2 sc.

Yarn over and pull through to fasten off, leaving a tail for sewing.

Back Legs (Make 2)

Rnd 1: Start 6 sc in an adjustable ring—6 sts.

Rnds 2–3: Sc in all 6 sts—6 sts.

Rnd 4: In FLO: (sc 1, ch 3, sl st in same st) 6 times.

Rnd 5: In back loops remaining from Rnd 2: sc in all 6 sts—6 sts.

Rnd 6: Sc in all 6 sts.

Do not fasten off or stuff; remove marker, press flat and close top with 2 sc.

Yarn over and pull through to fasten off, leaving a tail for sewing.

Tail

Rnd 1: Start 5 sc in an adjustable ring—5 sts.

Rnds 2–3: Sc in all 5 sts—5 sts.

Rnd 4: In FLO: (sc 1, ch 3, sl st in same st) 5 times.

Rnd 5: In back loops remaining from Rnd 2: sc in all 5 sts—5 sts.

Rnd 6: Sc in all 5 sts.

Do not fasten off or stuff; remove marker, press flat, and close top with 2 sc.

Yarn over and pull through to fasten off, leaving a tail for sewing.

ASSEMBLY

Attach the head to the body as shown.

After head is attached to body, sew on the remainder of the parts in whichever order you choose.

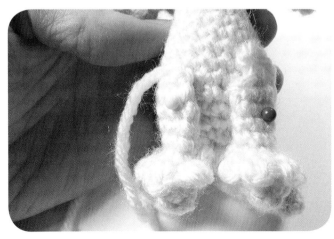

buck

Breed: Pug

Perpetually grumpy, Blossom's younger brother Buck seems to be going through some kind of identity crisis. He's always been the nostalgic type, as evidenced by his collection of old vinyl records and his brief Civil War reenactment phase. Lately he has taken to obsessing over the Cretaceous period and refuses to take off his dinosaur costume.

FINISHED SIZE: 2½in/6.5cm tall

SKILL LEVEL: Intermediate

MATERIALS

- Lion Brand® Vanna's Choice® 3.5oz/100g, 170yds/156m (100% acrylic)—one skein each: #860-126 Chocolate (Color A), #860-123 Beige (Color B), #860-175 Radiant Lime (Color C), #860-147 Purple (Color D)
- Size D-3 (3.25mm) crochet hook
- Yarn needle
- Embroidery needle
- Black embroidery floss (for eyes and nose)
- Polyester stuffing
- Wooden stuffing stick
- Stitch markers and pins

Head and Body

Head and body are started in Color A. **Sections shown in purple are completed in Color D.** *See "Changing Colors" in the Techniques section for more information on how to change yarn colors.*

In Color A, except where noted:

Rnd 1: Ch 3. Starting in second ch from hook, sc 1. In next st, sc 4. On opposite side of foundation ch, sc 4 into next st—9 sts.

Rnd 2: Sc 2, inc, sc 3 into next st, sc 3, sc 3 into next st, inc—15 sts.

Rnd 3: Sc in all 15 sts—15 sts.

Rnd 4: Change to Color B in first st. Sl st in all 15 sts—15 sts. Make sure to work each sl st loosely so you can work into them more easily in the next rounds.

Rnd 5: Sl st 5, sc 9, sc 3 into last st—17 sts.

Rnd 6: (Sc 3 into next st) 5 times, sc 12—27 sts.

Rnd 7: Sc in all 27 sts—27 sts. Embroider nose, eyes, and eyebrows.

Rnd 8: Sc 3, inc, sc 6, inc, sc 7, inc, sc 8—30 sts.

Rnd 9: Change to Color C in first st. Sc in all 30 sts—30 sts.

Rnd 10: In FLO: sc in all 30 sts—30 sts.

Rnd 11: In leftover back loops remaining from Rnd 10: Sc in all 30 sts—30 sts.

Rnd 12: Sc in all 30 sts—30 sts.

Rnd 13: Sc 7, inc, sc 14, inc, sc 7—32 sts.

Rnds 14–15: Sc in all 32 sts—32 sts.

Rnd 16: Sc 4, **sc 1**, sc 10, **sc 1**, sc 16—32 sts.

Rnd 17: Sc 2, **sc 1**, sc 3, **sc 1**, sc 2, **sc 1**, sc 3, **sc 1**, sc 4, **sc 1**, sc 13—32 sts.

Rnd 18: Sc 4, **sc 1**, sc 3, (**sc 1**, sc 3) 2 times, **sc 1**, sc 15—32 sts.

Rnd 19: Sc 7, dec, sc 14, dec, sc 7—30 sts.

Rnd 20: (Sc 3, dec) 6 times—24 sts. Begin stuffing the body generously, continuing to stuff firmly as you finish the following rounds.

Rnd 21: Sc 1, dec, (sc 2, dec) 5 times, sc 1—18 sts.

Rnd 22: (Sc 1, dec) 6 times—12 sts.

Rnd 23: Dec 6 times—6 sts.

Fasten off with a sl st, leaving a tail. Using a yarn needle, thread the tail through each of the front loops of the remaining 6 sts, pulling tightly to close hole. Weave in and trim yarn.

Dinosaur Tail

In Color C:

Rnd 1: Start 5 sc in an adjustable ring—5 sts.

Rnd 2: Sc 1, inc, sc 3—6 sts.

Rnd 3: Sc 2, inc 2 times, sc 2—8 sts.

Rnd 4: Sc in all 8 sts—8 sts.

Rnd 5: Sc 3, inc 3 times, sc 2—11 sts.

Rnd 6: Sc in all 11 sts—11 sts.

Fasten off with a sl st, leaving a tail for assembly. Stuff lightly.

Dinosaur Spikes

In Color D:

Row 1: Ch 13, making sure to leave a long tail (8in) while making your slipknot.

Row 2: Starting in second ch from hook, (sl st 2 times, ch 2) 6 times.

Yarn over and pull through to fasten off, leaving a tail for sewing.

Ears (Make 2)

In Color A:

Rnd 1: Start 5 sc in an adjustable ring—5 sts.

Rnd 2: Sc in all 5 sts—5 sts.

Do not fasten off or stuff; remove marker, press flat and close top with 2 sc. Yarn over and pull through to fasten off, leaving a tail for sewing.

Legs (Make 4):

In Color B:

Rnd 1: Start 5 sc in an adjustable ring—5 sts.

Rnd 2: Sc in all 5 sts—5 sts.

Fasten off with a sl st, leaving a tail for assembly. Do not stuff.

ASSEMBLY

Sew dinosaur tail to body as shown.

After tail is attached to body, sew on the remainder of the parts in whichever order you choose.

duncan

Breed: Golden Retriever

As one of the younger pups in the house, Duncan has lots of excess energy. He is ridiculously loud, running into walls and knocking things over as he runs. Some of the older pups have asked him to tone it down a bit, so he began wearing a bunny costume because bunnies are quiet and soft, right? It doesn't work, of course. He's just as noisy as always, maybe even more so!

FINISHED SIZE: 2½in/6.5cm tall (to top of body), 4½in/11.5cm tall (to top of bunny ears)

SKILL LEVEL: Intermediate

MATERIALS

- Lion Brand® Vanna's Choice® 3.5oz/100g, 170yds/156m (100% acrylic)—one skein each: #860-130 Honey (Color A), #860-100 White (Color B)
- Size D-3 (3.25mm) crochet hook
- Yarn needle
- Embroidery needle
- Black embroidery floss (for eyes and nose)
- Polyester stuffing
- Wooden stuffing stick
- Stitch markers and pins

Rnds 11–14: Sc in all 36 sts—36 sts. Embroider eyes and nose.

Head and Body

In Color A:

Rnd 1: Ch 4. Starting in second ch from hook, sc 2. In next st, sc 4. On opposite side of foundation ch, sc 1, sc 4 into next st—11 sts.

Rnds 2–3: Sc in all 11 sts—11 sts.

Rnd 4: (Sc 3 into next st) 4 times, (sc 1, inc) 3 times, sc 1—22 sts.

Rnd 5: Sc in all 22 sts—22 sts.

Rnd 6: Sc 1, (sc 3 into next st, sc 2) 4 times, sc 9—30 sts.

Rnd 7: Sc in all 30 sts—30 sts.

Change to Color B. The remainder of the rnds are worked in Color B.

Rnd 8: Sc 2, (inc, sc 3) 5 times, sc 4, inc, sc 3—36 sts.

Rnd 9: In FLO: sc in all 36 sts—36 sts.

Rnd 10: In leftover back loops remaining from Rnd 9: sc in all 36 sts—36 sts.

Rnd 15: (Sc 11, inc) 3 times—39 sts.

Rnd 16: Sc 6, inc, (sc 12, inc) 2 times, sc 6—42 sts.

Rnds 17–18: Sc in all 42 sts—42 sts.

Rnd 19: (Sc 5, dec) 6 times—36 sts.

Rnd 20: Sc 2, dec, (sc 4, dec) 5 times, sc 2—30 sts. Begin stuffing the body generously, continuing to stuff firmly as you finish the following rounds.

Rnd 21: (Sc 3, dec) 6 times—24 sts.

Rnd 22: Sc 1, dec, (sc 2, dec) 5 times, sc 1—18 sts.

Rnd 23: (Sc 1, dec) 6 times—12 sts.

Rnd 24: Dec 6 times—6 sts.

Fasten off with a sl st, leaving a tail. Using a yarn needle, thread the tail through each of the front loops of the remaining 6 sts, pulling tightly to close hole. Weave in and trim yarn.

Bunny Ears (Make 2)

In Color B:

Rnd 1: Start 6 sc in an adjustable ring—6 sts.

Rnd 2: (Sc 2, inc) 2 times—8 sts.

Rnds 3–5: Sc in all 8 sts—8 sts.

Rnd 6: Sc 2, dec, sc 4—7 sts.

Rnds 7–8: Sc in all 7 sts—7 sts.

Do not fasten off or stuff; remove marker, press flat, and close top with 3 sc. Yarn over and pull through to fasten off, leaving a tail for sewing.

Puppy Ears (Make 2)

In Color A:

Rnd 1: Start 6 sc in an adjustable ring—6 sts.

Rnd 2: (Sc 2, inc) 2 times—8 sts.

Rnd 3: Sc in all 8 sts—8 sts.

Rnd 4: (Sc 2, dec) 2 times— 6 sts.

Do not fasten off or stuff; remove marker, press flat, and close top with 2 sc. Yarn over and pull through to fasten off, leaving a tail for sewing.

Legs (Make 4)

In Color A:

Rnd 1: Start 6 sc in an adjustable ring—6 sts.

Rnds 2–3: Sc in all 6 sts—6 sts.

Fasten off with a sl st, leaving a tail for assembly. Do not stuff.

Tail (Make 2, then join)

In Color A:

Row 1: Ch 7, making sure to leave a long tail (8in) while making your slipknot.

Row 2: Starting in second ch from hook, sc 2, hdc 4.

Yarn over and pull through to fasten off, leaving a tail for sewing. Sandwich the two tail pieces together so the stitches are aligned, as shown at top of next page, and use one of the remaining tails to whipstitch the pieces together, down both sides.

Weave in and trim remaining tails, leaving one for assembly later.

ASSEMBLY

Parts can be assembled in whichever order you choose, as shown.

1. Position for puppy ears.

2. Position for bunny ears.

cardboard box

FINISHED SIZE: 2¼in/5.5cm by 3¾in/9.5cm

SKILL LEVEL: Easy

MATERIALS

• Lion Brand® Vanna's Choice® 3.5oz/100g, 170yds/156m (100% acrylic)—one skein: #860-130 Honey (Color A)

• Size D-3 (3.25mm) crochet hook

• Yarn needle

• Stitch marker

Box Bottom

Row 1: Ch 17. Starting in second ch from hook, sc 16. Ch 1 and turn—16 sts.

Rows 2–18: Sc in each st across. Ch 1 and turn—16 sts.

Fasten off. Turn piece clockwise and insert hook into st as shown.

Join new piece of yarn and sc 1 in this stitch, insert marker and continue.

Sc across edge of box for 16 sts.

Sc 3 into next (17th) st.

Sc in next 14 sts.

Sc 3 into next (15th) st.

Sc in next 15 sts.

Sc 3 into next (16th) st. Sc in next 14 sts. In 15th st, sc 3—71 sts.

You've now reached the marker. Proceed to work in rounds, beginning in the st with the marker:

Rnd 1: In BLO: sc in each st—71 sts.

Rnds 2–14: Sc in each st—71 sts.

Box Flaps (Make 4)

Row 1: Ch 17. Starting in second ch from hook, sc 16. Ch 1 and turn.

Rows 2–9: Sc in each st across. Ch 1 and turn—16 sts.

Do not fasten off. Sc around the perimeter of the flap, along the edges, until you have worked around the entire piece once. Fasten off and leave a tail for sewing.

ASSEMBLY

Use leftover tails to whipstitch flaps to top of cardboard box.

mack

Breed: Bulldog

When Wendy isn't hogging the television with her horror movie marathons, Mack is watching wrestling—and studying it with an unsettling intensity. Be careful when you're around him: he has big dreams of his own and won't hesitate to try out his signature body-slam move (the Mack Attack) on you. Ouch!

FINISHED SIZE: 3in/7.5cm tall

SKILL LEVEL: Intermediate

MATERIALS

- Lion Brand® Vanna's Choice® 3.5oz/100g, 170yds/156m (100% acrylic)—one skein each: #860-400 Oatmeal (Color A), #860-124 Toffee (Color B)
- Size D-3 (3.25mm) crochet hook
- Yarn needle
- Embroidery needle
- Black embroidery floss (for eyes, nose, and mouth)
- Polyester stuffing
- Wooden stuffing stick
- Stitch markers and pins

Muzzle

In Color A:

Rnd 1: Ch 4. Starting in second ch from hook, sc 2. In next st, sc 4. On opposite side of foundation ch, sc 1, sc 4 into next st—11 sts.

Rnd 2: Sc 3, sc 3 into next st, inc, sc 4, inc, sc 3 in next st—17 sts.

Rnd 3: Sc 4, inc, (sc 5, inc) 2 times—20 sts.

Rnd 4: Sc in all 20 sts—20 sts.

Fasten off with a sl st, leaving a tail for assembly. Embroider nose and mouth.

Head

Head is started in Color A. Sections shown in blue are worked in Color B. See "Changing Colors" in the Techniques section for more information on how to change yarn colors.

In Color A, except where noted:

Rnd 1: Ch 4. Starting in second ch from hook, sc 2. In next st, sc 4. On opposite side of foundation ch, sc 1, sc 4 into next st—11 sts.

Rnd 2: Sc 3, sc 3 into next st, inc, sc 2, sc 2, inc, sc 3 into next st—17 sts.

Rnd 3: (Sc 3, inc) 2 times, sc 2, sc 1, inc, sc 3, inc, sc 1—21 sts.

Rnd 4: Sc 2, inc, sc 4, inc, sc 4, inc, sc 4, inc, sc 3—25 sts.

Rnd 5: (Sc 4, inc) 2 times, sc 4, inc, (sc 4, inc) 2 times—30 sts.

Rnds 6–8: Sc 16, sc 14—30 sts. Remainder of rnds are completed in Color A.

Rnds 9–10: Sc in all 30 sts—30 sts. Embroider eyes.

Note: Pin muzzle to head temporarily to determine best eye placement.

Rnd 11: (Sc 3, dec) 6 times—24 sts. Begin stuffing the head generously, continuing to stuff firmly as you finish the following rounds.

Rnd 12: Sc 1 dec, (sc 2, dec) 5 times, sc 1—18 sts.

Rnd 13: (Sc 1, dec) 6 times—12 sts.

Rnd 14: Dec 6 times—6 sts.

Fasten off with a sl st, leaving a tail. Using a yarn needle, thread the tail through each of the front loops of the remaining 6 sts, pulling tightly to close hole. Weave in and trim yarn.

Body

Body is started in Color B. **Sections bolded in purple** *are completed in Color A. See "Changing Colors" in the Techniques section for more information on how to change yarn colors.*

In Color B, except where noted:

Rnd 1: Ch 4. Starting in second ch from hook, sc 2, (in next st, sc 2, **sc 2**), **on other side of foundation ch, sc 1,** (in next st, sc 3, sc 1)—11 sts.

Rnd 2: Sc 3, inc, **sc 3 into next st, sc 4, sc 3 into next st,** inc—17 sts.

Rnd 3: Sc 1, inc, sc 2, inc, **(sc 2, inc) 3 times, sc 1,** sc 1, sc 3 into last st—24 sts.

Rnd 4: Sc 3, inc, sc 3, **inc, (sc 3, inc) 3 times,** sc 3, inc—30 sts.

Rnd 5: Sc 8, **sc 1, inc, sc 9, inc, sc 5,** sc 4, inc—33 sts.

Rnd 6: Sc 8, **sc 1, dec, sc 9, dec, sc 5,** sc 4, dec—30 sts.

Rnd 7: Sc 4, dec, **sc 2, sc 6, dec, sc 7, dec,** sc 5—27 sts.

Rnd 8: Sc 7, **dec, sc 7, dec, sc 4,** sc 3, dec—24 sts.

Rnds 9–10: Sc 7, **sc 13,** sc 4—24 sts.

Fasten off with a sl st, leaving a tail for assembly. Stuff lightly.

Ears (Make 2)

Make one in Color A and one in Color B:

Rnd 1: Start 5 sc in an adjustable ring—5 sts.

Rnd 2: Sc 1, inc, sc 3—6 sts.

Rnd 3: Sc in all 6 sts—6 sts.

Do not fasten off or stuff; remove marker, press flat and insert hook through both sides to close top with 2 sc. Yarn over and pull through to fasten off, leaving a tail for sewing.

Front Legs (Make 2)

In Color A:

Rnd 1: Start 6 sc in an adjustable ring—6 sts.

Rnds 2–3: Sc in all 6 sts—6 sts.

Do not fasten off or stuff; remove marker, press flat and insert hook through both sides to close top with 2 sc. Yarn over and pull through to fasten off, leaving a tail for sewing.

Back Legs (Make 2)

In Color A:

Rnd 1: Start 7 sc in an adjustable ring—7 sts.

Rnds 2–3: Sc in all 7 sts—7 sts.

Fasten off with a sl st, leaving a tail for assembly. Stuff lightly.

Tail

In Color B:

Row 1: Ch 4, making sure to leave a long tail (8in) while making your slipknot.

Row 2: Starting in second ch from hook, sc, (hdc 4 in next st) 2 times.

Yarn over and pull through to fasten off, leaving a tail for sewing.

ASSEMBLY

Attach the head to the body as shown.

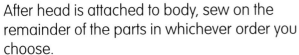

After head is attached to body, sew on the remainder of the parts in whichever order you choose.

dog🦴bone

Bonus Pattern!

FINISHED SIZE: 1½in/4cm long

SKILL LEVEL: Easy

MATERIALS

- Lion Brand® Vanna's Choice® 3.5oz/100g, 170yds/156m (100% acrylic)—one skein: #860-100 White
- Size D-3 (3.25mm) crochet hook
- Yarn needle
- Stitch marker

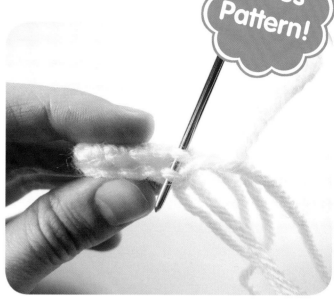

Bone, Center Portion (Make 2, then join)

In Color A:

Row 1: Ch 6, making sure to leave a long tail (8in) while making your slipknot.

Row 2: Starting in second ch from hook, sc 5.

Yarn over and pull through to fasten off, leaving a tail for sewing. Sandwich the two pieces together so the sts are aligned, as shown, and use one of the remaining tails to whipstitch the pieces together, down both sides. Weave in and trim remaining tails.

Bone, Ends (Make 4)

In Color A:

Row 1: Ch 3. In third ch from hook, hdc 4. Drop loop from hook, loosen loop. Reinsert hook into first of the 4 hdc sts, pick up dropped loop and pull it through. This creates a small cluster of sts in a ball shape.

Yarn over and pull through to fasten off.

ASSEMBLY

Assemble pieces as shown, weaving in and trimming extra yarn tails.

bruiser

Breed: Greyhound

Bruiser may look like the very image of canine grace with his aerodynamic frame and his long, elegant legs, but don't be fooled: he is the clumsiest pup in the house (maybe on the entire planet). His speed and lack of coordination make for a dangerous combination, and he's constantly coming inside with bumps and scratches. When you see him barreling your way, limbs flailing, watch out!

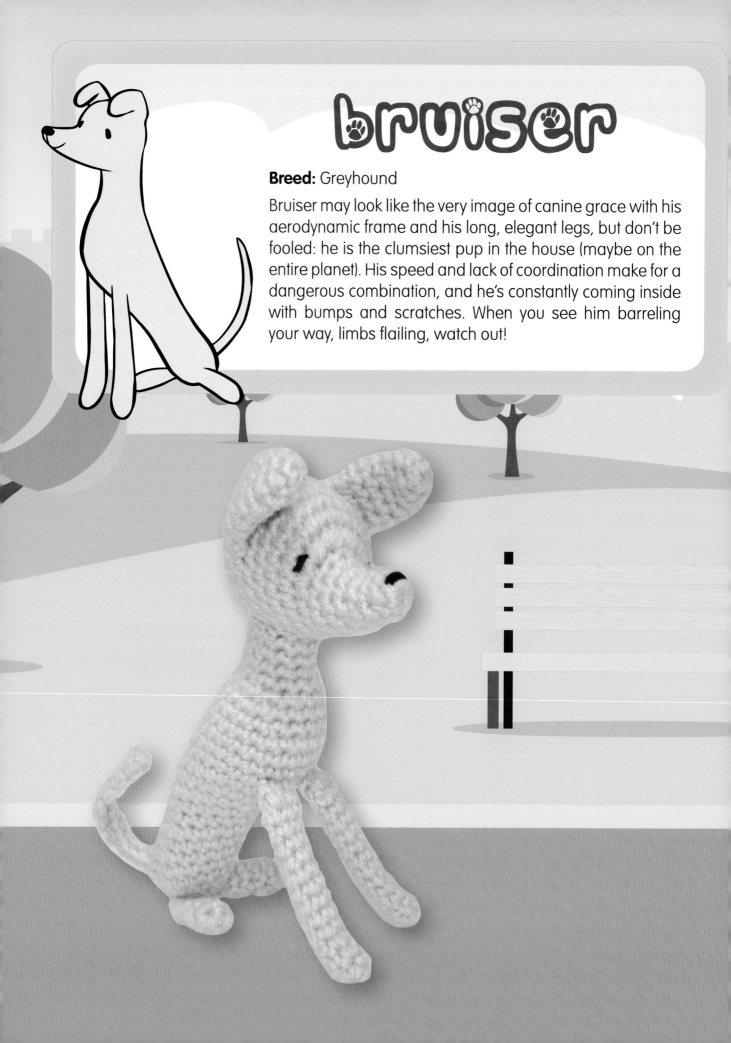

FINISHED SIZE: 6in/15cm tall

SKILL LEVEL: Intermediate

MATERIALS

- Lion Brand® Vanna's Choice® 3.5oz/100g, 170yds/156m (100% acrylic)—one skein: #860-123 Beige
- Size D-3 (3.25mm) crochet hook
- Yarn needle
- Embroidery needle
- Black embroidery floss (for eyes, nose, and mouth)
- Polyester stuffing
- Wooden stuffing stick
- Stitch markers and pins

Body

Rnd 1: Start 6 sc in an adjustable ring—6 sts.

Rnd 2: Inc 6 times—12 sts.

Rnd 3: (Sc 2, inc) 4 times—16 sts.

Rnd 4: Sc in all 16 sts—16 sts.

Rnd 5: Sc 1, (inc, sc 2) 3 times, dec 3 times—16 sts.

Rnd 6: Sc in all 16 sts—16 sts.

Rnd 7: Sc 3, (inc, sc 2) 3 times, dec 2 times—17 sts.

Rnd 8: Dec, sc 15—16 sts.

Rnd 9: Sc 4, (inc, sc 2) 3 times, dec.

There should be one st left in the round—remove marker and dec, replacing marker when dec is completed—17 sts.

Note: Dec counts as the first st of the next round.

Rnd 10: Dec, sc 14—16 sts.

Rnd 11: Sc 4, (inc, sc 2) 3 times, sc 3—19 sts.

Rnd 12: Dec, sc 4, (inc, sc 2) 3 times, sc 3. There should be one st left in the round—remove marker and dec, replacing marker when dec is completed—20 sts.

Rnd 13: Sc 4, (inc, sc 2) 4 times, sc 3—24 sts.

Rnd 14: Sc in all 24 sts—24 sts.

Rnd 15: Dec, sc 10, inc, sc 11—24 sts.

Rnd 16: Sc in all 24 sts—24 sts.

Rnd 17: Dec, sc 10, inc, sc 11—24 sts.

Rnd 18: Sc in all 24 sts—24 sts.

Rnd 19: Dec, sc 5, (dec, sc 2) 4 times, sc 1—19 sts.

Begin stuffing the body, continuing to stuff firmly as you finish the remaining rounds.

Rnd 20: Sc in all 19 sts—19 sts.

Rnd 21: Dec, (sc 3, dec) 2 times, sc 2, dec, sc 3—15 sts.

Rnd 22: (Sc 3, dec) 3 times—12 sts.

Rnd 23: Inc, sc 5, dec, sc 4—12 sts.

Rnds 24–25: Sc in all 12 sts—12 sts.

Fasten off with a sl st, leaving a tail for sewing.

Head

Rnd 1: Start 6 sc in an adjustable ring—6 sts.

Rnd 2: Sc in all 6 sts—6 sts.

Rnd 3: Sc 1, inc, sc 4—7 sts.

Rnd 4: Sc 3, inc, sc 3—8 sts.

Rnd 5: Sc 3, inc, sc 2, inc, sc 1—10 sts.

Rnd 6: Sc 3, inc, sc 3, inc, sc 2—12 sts.

Rnd 7: Sc 8, inc, sc 3—13 sts.

Rnd 8: Sc 6, inc, sc 3 into next 4 sts, inc, sc 1—23 sts.

Rnd 9: Sc 3, inc, sc 10, inc, sc 8—25 sts. Embroider nose.

Rnds 10–11: Sc in all 25 sts—25 sts.

Rnd 12: Sc 5, inc, sc 11, inc, sc 7—27 sts.

Rnd 13: Sc in all 27 sts—27 sts. Embroider eyes.

Front Legs (Make 2)

Rnd 1: Start 6 sc in an adjustable ring—6 sts.

Rnds 2–12: Sc in all 6 sts—6 sts.

Do not fasten off or stuff; remove marker, press flat and insert hook through both sides to close top with 2 sc. Yarn over and pull through to fasten off, leaving a tail for sewing.

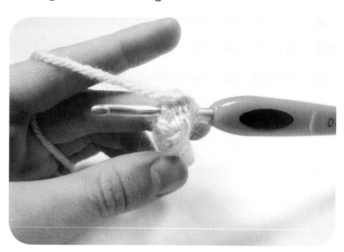

Rnd 14: Sc 4, dec, (sc 5, dec) 3 times—23 sts.

Rnd 15: (Sc 4, dec) 3 times, sc 3, dec—19 sts.

Begin stuffing the head, continuing to stuff firmly as you finish the remaining rounds.

Rnd 16: Sc 2, dec, (sc 3, dec) 3 times—15 sts.

Rnd 17: (Sc 1, dec) 5 times—10 sts.

Rnd 18: Dec 5 times—5 sts.

Fasten off with a sl st, leaving a tail. Using a yarn needle, thread the tail through each of the front loops of the remaining 5 sts, pulling tightly to close hole. Weave in and trim yarn.

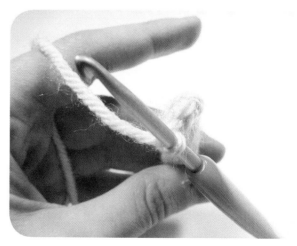

Back Legs (Make 2)

Rnd 1: Start 6 sc in an adjustable ring—6 sts.

Rnds 2–4: Sc in all 6 sts—6 sts.

Do not fasten off or stuff; remove marker, press flat and insert hook through both sides to close top with 2 sc. Yarn over and pull through to fasten off, leaving a tail for sewing.

Ears (Make 2)

Rnd 1: Start 5 sc in an adjustable ring—5 sts.

Rnd 2: Sc 1, inc, sc 3—6 sts.

Rnd 3: (Sc 2, inc) 2 times—8 sts.

Rnd 4: Sc in all 8 sts—8 sts.

Rnd 5: Sc 3, inc, sc 4—9 sts.

Rnds 6–7: Sc in all 9 sts—9 sts.

Do not fasten off or stuff; remove marker, press flat and insert hook through both sides to close top with 4 sc. Yarn over and pull through to fasten off, leaving a tail for sewing.

Tail

Row 1: Ch 13, making sure to leave a long tail (8in) while making your slipknot.

Row 2: Starting in second ch from hook, sc 12.

Yarn over and pull through to fasten off, leaving a tail for sewing.

ASSEMBLY

Attach the head to the body as shown.

After head is attached to body, sew on the remainder of the parts in whichever order you choose.

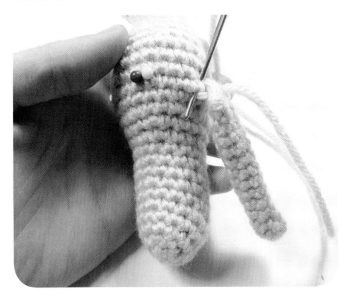

morty

Breed: French Bulldog

Beware the second floor guest bedroom! Morty likes to hang out underneath the bed in there to read his comic books. That would be fine, except the only thing Morty enjoys more than reading under the bed is hiding and waiting for people to walk by so he can pop out and scare them.

FINISHED SIZE: 3½in/9cm tall

SKILL LEVEL: Intermediate

MATERIALS

- Lion Brand® Vanna's Choice® 3.5oz./100g, 170yds/156m (100% acrylic)—one skein each: #860-123 Beige (Color A), #860-106 Aquamarine (Color B), #860-153 Black (Color C), #860-100 White (Color D), #860-175 Radiant Lime (Color E), #860-147 Purple (Color F)

- Size D-3 (3.25mm) crochet hook

- Yarn needle

- Embroidery needle

- Black embroidery floss (for eyes, nose, and mouth)

- Polyester stuffing

- Wooden stuffing stick

- Stitch markers and pins

Muzzle

In Color A:

Rnd 1: Ch 4. Starting in second ch from hook, sc 2. In next st, sc 4. On opposite side of foundation ch, sc 1, sc 4 into next st—11 sts.

Rnd 2: Sc 3, inc, sc 3 in next st, sc 4, sc 3 in next st, inc—17 sts.

Fasten off with a sl st, leaving a tail for assembly. Embroider nose.

Head

In Color A:

Rnd 1: Ch 4. Starting in second ch from hook, sc 2. In next st, sc 4. On opposite side of foundation ch, sc 1, sc 4 into next st—11 sts.

Rnd 2: Sc 3, inc, sc 3 in next st, sc 4, sc 3 in next st, inc—17 sts.

Rnd 3: Sc 4, inc 3 times, sc 6, inc 3 times, sc 1—23 sts.

Rnd 4: Sc 3 in next st, sc 2, sc 3 in next st, sc 19—27 sts.

Rnd 5: Sc in all 27 sts, changing to Color B in last st—27 sts.

Rnd 6: Sc in all 27 sts—27 sts.

Rnd 7: In FLO: sc in all 27 sts—27 sts.

Rnd 8: In leftover back loops remaining from Rnd 7: sc 1, inc, (sc 4, inc) 2 times, sc 11, inc, sc 3—31 sts.

Rnds 9–10: Sc in all 31 sts—31 sts.

Pin muzzle to head to determine eye placement and embroider eyes. Using Color D, embroider monster fangs as shown.

Rnd 11: Sc 4, dec, sc 8, dec, sc 12, dec, sc 1—28 sts.

Rnd 12: (Sc 5, dec) 4 times—24 sts. Begin stuffing the head, continuing to stuff firmly as you finish the remaining rounds.

Rnd 13: Sc 2, dec, (sc 4, dec) 3 times, sc 2—20 sts.

Rnd 14: Dec 10 times—10 sts.

Rnd 15: Dec 5 times—5 sts.

Fasten off with a sl st, leaving a tail. Using a yarn needle, thread the tail through each of the front loops of the remaining 5 sts, pulling tightly to close hole. Weave in and trim yarn.

Body

In Color A:

Rnd 1: Ch 5. Starting in second ch from hook, sc 3, sc 4 in next st. On opposite side of foundation ch, sc 2, sc 4 into next st—13 sts.

Rnd 2: Sc 4, inc, sc 3 in next st, sc 5, sc 3 in next st, inc—19 sts.

Rnd 3: Inc, sc 3, inc, sc 4, inc, sc 3, inc, sc 5—23 sts.

Rnd 4: Dec, sc 3, dec, sc 4, dec, sc 3, dec, sc 5, changing to Color B in last st—19 sts.

Rnd 5: Sc in all 19 sts—19 sts.

Rnd 6: In FLO: sc in all 19 sts—19 sts.

Rnd 7: In leftover back loops remaining from Rnd 6, sc in all 19 sts—19 sts.

Rnd 8: Sc 2, dec, sc 7, dec, sc 6—17 sts.

Rnd 9: Sc in all 17 sts—17 sts.

Fasten off with a sl st, leaving a tail for sewing. Stuff lightly.

Front Legs (Make 2)

In Color A:

Rnd 1: Start 5 sc in an adjustable ring—5 sts.

Rnd 2: Sc in all 5 sts, changing to Color B in last st—5 sts.

Rnds 3–5: Sc in all 5 sts—5 sts.

Do not fasten off or stuff; remove marker, press flat and insert hook through both sides to close top with 2 sc. Yarn over and pull through to fasten off, leaving a tail for sewing.

Back Legs (Make 2)

In Color A:

Rnd 1: Start 5 sc in an adjustable ring—5 sts.

Rnds 2–3: Sc in all 5 sts—5 sts.

Do not fasten off or stuff; remove marker, press flat and insert hook through both sides to close top with 2 sc. Yarn over and pull through to fasten off, leaving a tail for sewing.

Monster Eyes (Make 2)

In Color C:

Rnd 1: Start 6 sc in an adjustable ring—6 sts.

Rnd 2: Change to Color D in first st. (Sc 1, inc) 3 times—9 sts.

Rnd 3: Sc in all 9 sts—9 sts.

Fasten off with a sl st, leaving a tail for sewing. Do not stuff.

Horns (Make 2)

In Color E:

Rnd 1: Start 4 sc in an adjustable ring—4 sts.

Rnd 2: Sc 1, inc, sc 2—5 sts.

Rnd 3: Sc 1, inc, sc 3, changing to Color F in last st—6 sts.

Rnd 4: (Sc 2, inc) 2 times—8 sts.

Rnd 5: Sc in all 8 sts, changing to Color E in last st—8 sts.

Rnd 6: (Sc 3, inc) 2 times—10 sts.

Rnd 7: Sc in all 10 sts—10 sts.

Fasten off with a sl st, leaving a tail for sewing. Stuff lightly.

ASSEMBLY

Assemble in the following order:

1. Pin head to body and join, adding extra stuffing as you work.

2. Sew back legs to bottom of body.

3. Sew front legs to front of body between Rnds 6–7.

4. Sew monster eyes to top of cap.

5. Sew horns to monster cap.

cole

Breed: Black Labrador Retriever (Black Lab)

With his dark fur and his big frame, Cole can be quite the intimidating pup. When he's out in the yard, strangers go bolting in the other direction when they see him run up to the fence—which breaks his heart! All Cole wants to do is chat with passersby and make small talk, so he has started dressing up as the least threatening-looking thing possible. The costume is working pretty well for him since everyone (especially the kids) seems to love unicorns.

FINISHED SIZE: 6½in/16.5cm talll

SKILL LEVEL: Intermediate

MATERIALS

- Lion Brand® Vanna's Choice® 3.5oz/100g, 170yds/156m (100% acrylic)—one skein each: #860-404 Dark Gray Heather (Color A), #860-115 Light Blue (Color B), #860-159 Lemon (Color C), #860-104 Pink Grapefruit (Color D), #860-183, Periwinkle (Color E)
- Size D-3 (3.25mm) crochet hook
- Size C (2.5mm) crochet hook
- Wire slicker brush (can be found in most pet stores)
- Yarn needle
- Embroidery needle
- Gray embroidery floss (for eyes and nose)
- Polyester stuffing
- Wooden stuffing stick
- Stitch markers and pins

Ears (Make 2)

In Color A:

Rnd 1: Start 6 sc in an adjustable ring—6 sts.

Rnd 2: (Sc 1, inc) 3 times—9 sts.

Rnd 3: (Sc 2, inc) 3 times—12 sts.

Rnd 4: Sc in all 12 sts—12 sts.

Rnd 5: (Sc 2, dec) 3 times—9 sts.

Rnd 6: Sc in all 9 sts—9 sts.

Rnd 7: (Sc 1, dec) 3 times—6 sts.

Do not fasten off or stuff; press flat and close top with 3 sc. Yarn over and pull through to fasten off, leaving a tail for sewing.

Muzzle

In Color A:

Rnd 1: Ch 4. Starting in second ch from hook, sc 2. In next st, sc 4. On opposite side of foundation ch, sc 1, sc 4 into next st—11 sts.

Rnd 2: Sc 3, sc 3 into next st, inc, sc 4, inc, sc 3 into next st—17 sts.

Rnds 3–4: Sc in all 17 sts—17 sts.

Fasten off with a sl st, leaving a tail for assembly. Embroider nose.

Head

In Color A:

Rnd 1: Ch 5. Starting in second ch from hook, sc in next 3 sts. In next st, sc 4. On opposite side of foundation ch, sc 2, sc 4 into next st—13 sts.

Rnd 2: Sc 4, sc 3 into next st, inc, sc 5, inc, sc 3 into next st—19 sts.

Rnd 3: (Sc 2, inc) 6 times, sc 1—25 sts.

Rnd 4: (Sc 3, inc) 6 times, sc 1—31 sts.

Rnd 5: Sc 2, inc, (sc 4, inc) 5 times, sc 2, inc—38 sts.

Rnd 6: (Sc 4, inc) 2 times, sc 30—40 sts.

Rnds 7–8: Sc in all 40 sts, changing to Color B in last st of Rnd 8—40 sts.

Rnd 9: (Sc 9, inc) 4 times—44 sts.

Rnd 10: In FLO: sc in all 44 sts—44 sts.

Rnd 11: In leftover back loops remaining from Rnd 10, sc 5, inc, (sc 10, inc) 3 times, sc 5—48 sts.

Rnds 12–14: Sc in all 48 sts—48 sts.

Pin muzzle to head to determine eye placement and embroider eyes.

Rnd 15: (Sc 23, inc) 2 times—50 sts.

Rnd 16: Sc in all 50 sts—50 sts.

Rnd 17: Sc 4, dec, (sc 8, dec) 4 times, sc 4—45 sts.

Rnd 18: (Sc 7, dec) 5 times—40 sts.

Rnd 19: Sc 3, dec, (sc 6, dec) 4 times, sc 3—35 sts.

Rnd 20: (Sc 5, dec) 5 times—30 sts. Begin stuffing the head, continuing to stuff firmly as you finish the remaining rounds.

Rnd 21: Sc 2, dec, (sc 4, dec) 4 times, sc 2—25 sts.

Rnd 22: (Sc 3, dec) 5 times—20 sts.

Rnd 23: Dec 10 times—10 sts.

Rnd 24: Dec 5 times—5 sts.

Fasten off with a sl st, leaving a tail. Using a yarn needle, thread the tail through each of the front loops of the remaining 5 sts, pulling tightly to close hole. Weave in and trim yarn.

Body

In Color A:

Rnd 1: Ch 4. Starting in second ch from hook, sc 2, sc 4 into next st. On opposite side of foundation ch, sc 1, sc 4 into next st—11 sts.

Rnd 2: Sc 3, sc 3 into next st, inc, sc 4, inc, sc 3 in next st—17 sts.

Rnd 3: Sc 4, inc in next 3 sts, sc 6, inc in next 3 sts, sc 1—23 sts.

Rnd 4: Sc 5, (inc, sc 1) 3 times, sc 6, (inc, sc 1) 3 times—29 sts.

Rnd 5: Sc 6, (inc, sc 2) 3 times, sc 5, (inc, sc 2) 3 times—35 sts.

Rnd 6: Sc 7, (inc, sc 3) 3 times, sc 5, (inc, sc 3) 2 times, inc, sc 2—41 sts.

Rnd 7: Sc 7, (inc, sc 4) 3 times, sc 5, (inc, sc 4) 2 times, inc, sc 3—47 sts.

Rnd 8: Sc 8, (inc, sc 5) 3 times, sc 5, (inc, sc 5) 2 times, inc, sc 3—53 sts.

Rnds 9–10: Sc in all 53 sts—53 sts.

Rnd 11: Sc 8, (dec, sc 5) 3 times, sc 6, (dec, sc 5) 2 times, dec, sc 2—47 sts.

Rnd 12: Sc in all 47 sts—47 sts.

Rnd 13: Sc 14, dec, sc 13, dec, sc 14, dec—44 sts.

Rnds 14–15: Sc in all 44 sts—44 sts.

Rnd 16: Sc 6, dec, sc 19, dec, sc 13, dec—41 sts.

Rnd 17: Sc in all 41 sts—41 sts.

Rnd 18: Sc 12, dec, sc 11, dec, sc 12, dec—38 sts.

Rnd 19: Sc in all 38 sts—38 sts.

Rnd 20: Sc 5, dec, sc 17, dec, sc 10, dec—35 sts.

Rnd 21: In first st, change to Color B. Sc in all 35 sts—35 sts.

Rnd 22: In FLO: sc in all 35 sts—35 sts.

Rnd 23: In leftover back loops remaining from Rnd 22, sc in all 35 sts—35 sts.

Rnd 24: Sc 10, dec, sc 9, dec, sc 10, dec—32 sts.

Rnd 25: Sc in all 32 sts—32 sts.

Fasten off with a sl st, leaving a tail for sewing. Stuff lightly.

Back Legs (Make 2)

In Color A:

Rnd 1: Start 7 sc in an adjustable ring—7 sts.

Rnd 2: Inc 7 times—14 sts.

Rnds 3–6: Sc in all 14 sts—14 sts.

Fasten off with a sl st, leaving a tail for sewing. Stuff firmly.

Front Legs (Make 2)

In Color A:

Rnd 1: Start 6 sc in an adjustable ring—6 sts.

Rnd 2: (Sc 1, inc) 3 times—9 sts.

Rnds 3–6: Sc in all 9 sts—9 sts.

Do not fasten off. Stuff lightly, remove marker, press flat and insert hook through both sides to close top with 2 sc. Yarn over and pull through to fasten off, leaving a tail for sewing.

Tail (Make 2, then join)

In Color A:

Row 1: Ch 11, making sure to leave a long tail (12in) while making your slipknot.

Row 2: Starting in second ch from hook, sc 5, hdc 5.

Yarn over and pull through to fasten off, leaving a tail for sewing. Sandwich the two tail pieces together so the sts are aligned and use one of the remaining tails to whipstitch the pieces together, down both sides. Weave in and trim remaining tails, leaving one for assembly later.

Unicorn Ears (Make 2)

In Color B:

Rnd 1: Start 5 sc in an adjustable ring—5 sts.

Rnd 2: Sc 2, inc, sc 2—6 sts.

Rnd 3: (Sc 2, inc) 2 times—8 sts.

Rnd 4: (Sc 3, inc) 2 times—10 sts.

Rnd 5: Sc 2, dec, sc 4, dec, sc 2—12 sts.

Rnd 6: Sc in all 12 sts—12 sts.

Do not fasten off or stuff; remove marker, pinch together bottom of ear as shown and insert hook through both sides to close top with 3 sc. Yarn over and pull through to fasten off, leaving a tail for sewing.

Unicorn Horn

In Color C:

Rnd 1: Start 4 sc in an adjustable ring—4 sts.

Rnd 2: Sc 1, inc, sc 2—5 sts.

Rnd 3: Sc 1, inc, sc 3—6 sts.

Rnd 4: Sc 3, inc, sc 2—7 sts.

Rnd 5: Sc 5, inc, sc 1—8 sts.

Rnd 6: Sc 2, inc, sc 5—9 sts.

Rnd 7: Sc in all 9 sts—9 sts.

Fasten off with a sl st, leaving a tail for sewing. Stuff firmly.

ASSEMBLY

Attach the head to the body as shown, adding extra stuffing as you work.

After head is attached to body, sew on the remainder of parts in whichever order you choose, as shown.

Mane

Note: You will alternate 3 rows of colors D and E to create a striped mane.

After all of the pieces are assembled, using a Size C/2.5mm hook, insert your hook underneath the st on the back of the unicorn hood, as shown,

and draw up a piece of yarn about 8in long. Pull through and knot the yarn twice. Repeat in rows of 2–3 sts down the length of the head, alternating the colors. Don't worry if some rows have 2 sts and others have 3 sts. It won't be noticeable once you brush out the mane.

Using a wire slicker brush, carefully brush out the yarn until it becomes fuzzy. Trim again and style if desired.